BEYOND
JENNIFER

A N D

JASON

BEYOND
JENNIFER
AND
JASON

▶ An Enlightened Guide to
Naming Your Baby

BY LINDA ROSENKRANTZ AND PAMELA REDMOND SATRAN

ST. MARTIN'S PRESS/NEW YORK

BEYOND JENNIFER AND JASON. Copyright © 1988 by Linda Rosenkrantz and Pamela Redmond Satran. All rights reserved. Printed in the United States of America. No part of this book may be used or reproduced in any manner whatsoever without written permission except in the case of brief quotations embodied in critical articles or reviews. For information, address St. Martin's Press, 175 Fifth Avenue, New York, N.Y. 10010.

DESIGN BY GUENET ABRAHAM

Library of Congress Cataloging-in-Publication Data

Rosenkrantz, Linda.
    Beyond Jennifer and Jason : an enlightened guide to naming your baby / by Linda Rosenkrantz and Pamela Redmond Satran.
    p. cm.
    ISBN 0-312-01907-6   ISBN 0-312-01908-4 (pbk.)
    1. Names, Personal—United States.   I. Satran, Pamela Redmond.
II. Title.
CS2377.R67 1988   88-1840
929.4′4′0973—dc19

10 9 8 7 6 5 4 3 2

For our wonderful daughters
Chloe Samantha Finch
and
Rory Elizabeth Margaret Satran

CONTENTS

ACKNOWLEDGMENTS

Our first thanks go to our editor, Hope Dellon, for believing in this project and for bringing it to its perfect realization. Also, we want to thank our agent, Howard Morhaim, for his energy and enthusiasm. And special thanks to Nancy Fish for her early input and Joseph Redmond for his early encouragement; to Fred Krantz of the Wisconsin Department of Health and Social Services for his tremendous guidance in compiling statistics on most-popular names; to Roger Smith of the California Health Demographics Section and Tim Smith of the New York State Health Department for their help on popularity rankings; to Rabbi Mark Hurvitz for advice on Jewish naming traditions and Hebrew names; to Emily Shapiro for her help with Creative Class; to Rita DiMatteo for insights into Italian-American naming traditions; to Alison Acker, for her helpful suggestions; to the parents whose real-life considerations when naming their children provided inspiration for this book—Andrea and Alan Higbie, Marian Golan, Peter Richmond and Melissa Davis, Mary Jo Kochakian, Chuck and Jone Fulkerson, and Mary Jean Shalhoub; and finally thanks to our husbands, Christopher Finch and Richard Satran, for understanding the obsession.

INTRODUCTION

The first, most important, and most lasting gift you bestow on your baby is a name. The aim of this book is to lead you to the perfect choice for your child, a name with which your son or daughter can live happily ever after.

Most other name books consist of one long alphabetical list; *Beyond Jennifer and Jason* offers almost a hundred separate lists, designed both to awaken you to new possibilities and to narrow the focus of your own personal slate of candidates. Where other books tell you that Cameron means "crooked nose" in Scotch Gaelic and Rachel means "a female sheep" in Hebrew, this book deals with contemporary perceptions of these names in the preschool and the playground and beyond. Here you will find lists devoted to trendy names, fashionable names and names due for a revival, lists of names that project brains and those that project beauty, lists of boyish names for girls and macho names for boys, some surprising names of saints and names that follow the "kosher curve." In other words, you will find lists to guide you through every concern, satisfy every naming consideration you may have.

And we don't just abandon you to the lists; each is supported by pertinent information: How kids feel about having the same name as four of their friends, for instance, or what psychologists say about the effect of offbeat names. Which ambisexual names are becoming too girlish for boys, and what you should keep in mind about nicknames, middle names, and sibling names. What it's like for a boy to be a junior, and why you should think twice about naming your child after someone famous.

All the information you need to make an informed and felicitous choice is organized into four easy-to-follow sections:

Style: A look at popularity, fashion, and trends. Here's where you'll find details on which names are in, out, hot, not. Fresh names for the nineties. Also here: the only accurate list of most-popular names, the only comprehensive guide to what the rich, famous, and royal are naming their children.

Image: A guide to the impressions names project. In this section you'll find names with the power to evoke brains, creativity, energy, and beauty. Names with newfound class, names that will help your child both fit in and stand out, and names that may prove too much—or not enough—for your little one to live up to.

Sex: Signposts for negotiating the gender maze. Girls' names are divided into four groups, from ultrafeminine to boyish. Boys' names are categorized from macho to wimpy. And the ever widening pool of ambisexual names is organized for you from the most girlish to the almost exclusively male.

Tradition: A look at the history, the ethnic and religious meanings of names. Names that reflect your unique background, including hundreds of surprising and unusual choices. Also here: How to find a name you and your spouse both love (and why you may have trouble doing so); choosing a name with baby's brothers and sisters—existing or future—in mind.

A note on the spelling of names in this book: For the most part, we have used only the most classic spelling of each name. When more than one variation is listed (Catherine/Katherine, for example), it is because both spellings are equally proper and well-accepted.

It's possible to use this book for consultation on names you already know you like: to find out, for instance, whether Emily is considered classic or trendy, whether Whitney still has any masculine punch. Or you can start with the qualities most important to you and use this book to find names that satisfy them: to cull a list of selections that work for either a boy or girl, that sound energetic, that aren't too trendy, and that have Celtic roots, for example. We think the best way to read this book is as a whole, using a combination of the two techniques. When you find a category that appeals—Creative Power Names, say—choose specific examples you like and then check the index for other sections in which they appear.

And in the end, you'll have the pleasure of knowing you have made a thoughtful and enlightened choice, whether you decide to move beyond Jennifer and Jason or not.

STYLE

What do we mean by style in terms of naming your baby?

Ideally, we're talking about personal style: finding a name that reflects your taste, that moves beyond fad and fashion, yet succeeds in catching the sound and spirit of the age.

Your attitudes towards style in other aspects of your life—from clothing and furniture to the way you live and your vision of the world—will affect your judgments about style in names. Whether you're conservative or liberal, care about being in fashion or rebel against it, set trends or avoid them, will all influence the style of the name you choose.

Because style changes constantly, differentiating among the names that are trendy and those that are fashionable, the names that are due for a comeback and those that are hopelessly out of date, can be difficult. That's where this section can act as your guide.

First, we outline current style: the names being used by fashionable people right now. Many of these names may not be widely popular this year, but they're heading there.

Next, you'll find a comprehensive list of the names that have been topping popularity lists for the past few years. These are the trendy names, threatened by overexposure, that you may find so far in they're out. If some of your favorites appear on this list, take heart: We also offer a selection of fresher-sounding substitutes for Jennifer, Jason, and friends.

If your desire is to find a name in the vanguard of style, the lists for you are those in the chapter of names that are so far out they're in. These are the names we believe will set the fashions for the next decade and beyond.

And if you want to find a name that truly bucks fashion—or if you want to avoid the names that are hopelessly out of style—consult the list of names that are so far out they'll always be out.

You may want to compare the names you like with those the rest of the world is choosing. Here you'll find lists of the most popular names in the United States, as well as a comprehensive catalog of what the rich, famous, and royal have been naming their children. The celebrity section also includes names linked to real people and fictional characters—names as accessible as Ally, as off-limits as Oprah—and why you should think twice about letting a star's popularity be your naming guide.

WHAT'S HOT

The major naming trends of today have one thing in common: They're all tied to tradition. Cute names, made-up names, five-minute fads, and other flights of fancy are out. Names that sound as if they've been plucked from the family tree are in.

We've divided the currently stylish names into three categories: Nouveau Conservatif, Grandma and Grandpa, and Androgynous Executive.

You won't find most of these names on any popularity lists, as there is always a lag between the vanguard and more common use. Where you will find them is on birth announcements engraved at Tiffany's, on silver spoons delivered to Manhattan townhouses, and on the waiting lists for topflight nursery schools. You'll also see many of these names in the birth announcements noteworthy enough to be carried in *People* magazine or *Women's Wear Daily*.

Some of these fashionable names will endure, some will become so popular they'll spark trends of their own, and others will before long join the list of names that are so far in they're out.

While choosing one of these names may seem to be setting you and your child apart from the herd for the moment, you may just be hopping on another trend, albeit a newer and fresher one. Many of these names are interesting, attractive, serviceable. But if your main intention is to be different, to choose a name no one else is choosing, be warned. You could be picking a Jennifer or Jason of the future.

NOUVEAU CONSERVATIF NAMES

We live in an era of conservative chic. Things classic, traditional, and time-honored are held in esteem, and names are no exception. Nouveau Conservatif names—good, solid standards like Elizabeth and William—are in style right now, along with restored colonial houses, Ralph Lauren tweeds, and real oriental rugs.

The Nouveau Conservatif group is composed of names that last. They are the classics, fit for—and often bestowed upon—newborn princes and princesses. But just because these names have been used for ages does not mean they transcend trendiness. Rather, they're part of a trend to ignore what's trendy, to be different from everyone who's trying to be different.

As a result, some Nouveau Conservatif names—Elizabeth and William, for instance, along with Katherine and Charles—are becoming (although it seems a contradiction in terms) trendy. The fashionable way to use these names now is in their proper form only: Today's James is called James, never Jimmy or Jamie.

If you don't believe these classics could possibly have anything to do with style, consider some of the other classic names that haven't made the Nouveau Conservatif roster, like Richard or Mary. Becoming too popular at some point in recent memory (remember little Ricky and all his namesakes?) or too identified with any ethnic group (as Mary is now often perceived as primarily Catholic) knocks a name out of consideration for the Nouveau Conservatif list.

If you choose a Nouveau Conservatif name, rest assured that no one will ever call you a slave of fashion. But also be aware that neither are you necessarily choosing a name that is truly timeless: Even tweed jackets move in and out of style to some extent and today's Nouveau Conservatif could conceivably end up tomorrow's So Far Out It Will Always Be Out.

Nouveau conservatif names

G I R L S

ALICE
ANN(E)
CAROLINE
CATHERINE/
   KATHERINE
CHARLOTTE
CLAIRE
EDITH
ELIZABETH

GRACE
HOPE
JANE
JULIA
LOUISE
LUCY
MARGARET
MARTHA
SALLY

B O Y S

ANDREW
CHARLES

DANIEL
EDWARD

HENRY	PHIL(L)IP
JAMES	THOMAS
JOHN	WILLIAM
PETER	

GRANDMA AND GRANDPA NAMES

Grandma and Grandpa names are not pretty names. They are earthy as opposed to glossy, plain as opposed to fancy, humble as opposed to pretentious. In these ways they go as far beyond Jennifer and Jason as you can get.

Grandma and Grandpa names celebrate the beauty of the *hamish*, the unadorned, the ordinary. Theirs is the style of unfinished pine furniture, rag rugs, and hand-stitched quilts. There's a certain hipness in their rejection of all that glitters, as there is in a movie star who lives on a ranch instead of in Hollywood. These names don't try too hard; they don't really try at all. And therein lies the secret of their charm.

You will notice that several of the names on the Grandma and Grandpa list are nicknames. Many people are simply bestowing these familiar forms on their children—just plain Sam or Lizzie or Maggie. But others will choose a proper name—Samuel or Elizabeth or Margaret—for the sole purpose of getting the Grandma and Grandpa nickname. The advantage of going with the proper name, of course, is that if your little Lizzie grows up and decides she wants to be a commodities broker rather than a weaver, she has the option of calling herself Elizabeth. And although that time seems a long way off, Elizabeth will look more impressive than Lizzie on a job application.

If you choose a Grandma or Grandpa name for your child, you are probably looking for something out of the ordinary, a name that may never sound attractive enough to be trendy. Some parents of Sams and Maxes have told us they liked the names because they were too downright homely to be chosen by very many other people. Well, we have news for them. Just as Robert Redford, Sissy Spacek, and Jessica Lange have rejected Hollywood glamour and pretense by retreating to remote farms and ranches, so too are there lots of little Sams and Maxes ambling into the world. (See "So Far Out They're On Their Way In," page 21.)

If you really want a name that bucks the crowd, try Egbert. Now, that's ugly.

Grandma and grandpa names

G I R L S

ANNA	LIZZIE
ANNIE	MAGGIE
BECKY	MOLLY
BESS	NELL
CEIL	NORA
EMMA	ROSIE
FANNY	SADIE
GOLDIE	SARA(H)
HANNAH	SONIA
JENNY	SOPHIE
JESSIE	TESS
LEAH	TILLIE
LILY	WILLA

B O Y S

ABE	JOE
BEN	MAX
CHARLIE	NAT
CLEM	SAM
HARRY	SIMON
JACK	WILL
JAKE	

ANDROGYNOUS EXECUTIVE NAMES

Is it a boy? Is it a girl? Is it a future CEO? Nursery schools, colleges, and corporations will one day be wondering, but only the parents will know for sure.

Names we classify as Androgynous Executive—names sometimes used by preppies and Southerners in the past—were fostered by the feminist movement and promoted further by the corporate, competitive eighties. The current style is to use most of these names for girls rather than boys, as it is still considered more of an advantage for a girl to possess masculine qualities than for a boy to embody feminine ones. Of course, some of these names—Gordon, Reed, Tyler—have retained a distinctly masculine bent, and are still used mostly for boys. But others, such as Whitney, Page, and Ashley, are now thoroughly feminized, so their androgynous advantage—if you choose to see it as that—is fading.

For the most part, however, these are not boys' names or girls' names—they are surnames, patrician-sounding enough to confer upon a child an automatic pedigree. Whether you can really claim a Whitney or a Morgan as an ancestor doesn't matter: The objective is a well-bred image. Image is what sets these names apart from other ambisexual names like Casey or Jody. Giving a girl an Androgynous Executive name doesn't say you want her to be a cute little tomboy, but rather that you are looking ahead to her capable, forceful womanhood. For a boy, the image is slightly different: Yes, he's from the kind of family that could foot the bill for Harvard Business School if that's where he wanted to go, but he might just as easily choose to be a painter instead.

Examine the various branches of your own family tree. Great-grandma's maiden name or an uncle's middle name, hidden away on the pages of an old photograph album or family Bible, might make an original yet authentic first-name choice for your son or daughter.

Androgynous executive names

ABBOTT	CARSON
ADDISON	CARTER
AMORY	FARRELL
ARCHER	HARPER
ARDEN	JORDAN
AVERELL	KEIL
AVERY	KENDALL
BLAINE	KENYON
BLAIR	KIMBALL
BLAKE	KIRBY
BROOKS	KYLE
BROWN	LANE
CAMERON	MACKENZIE

MALLORY	PORTER
MORGAN	PRICE
NORRIS	REED
PA(I)GE	SCHUYLER
PALMER	SLOAN
PARKER	TAYLOR
PAXTON	TYLER
PEYTON	WALKER

SO FAR IN THEY'RE OUT

The whole issue of trendiness in names is a double-edged sword. For the most part, kids like having popular names; they like swimming in the mainstream. You wouldn't find many seven-year-old Samanthas, Seans, or Sams out there who would say they hated their names. On the other hand, there might be quite a few twenty-seven-year-old Sharis, Scotts, or Shelleys who would voice some regrets at being known to the world by those epidemic names of the sixties.

We present the following master list of So Far In They're Out names so that if you choose one of them for your child, it will be with the knowledge that these names carry with them this dilemma of trendiness. Even if there aren't any Brandons or Caitlins or Jesses on your block yet, it doesn't mean they aren't trendy names. As fresh as some of them may sound to your ear, there's a good chance that three other kids with the same name will be in your child's kindergarten class.

But what if Nicole is your favorite name despite its trendy status? Either forge ahead with it, knowing that your Nicole will bring something unique to the name, or consult the substitution guide that follows.

So far in they're out names

G I R L S

ALEXANDRA	ERICA
ALEXIS	ERIN
AL(L)ISON	HAYLEY/ HALEY
ALYSSA (and	HEATHER
variations like	HIL(L)ARY
ILISSA, ELICIA, et	JAMIE
al)	JENNIFER
AMANDA	JENNY
AMY	JESSICA
ANNIE	JESSIE
ARIEL	JORDAN
ASHLEY	KELLY
BETHANY	KIM
BRITTANY	KIMBERLY
BROOKE	KIRSTEN
CAITLIN	KRISTIN
CHRISSIE	LAUREN
CHRISTIE	LINDSAY/LINDSEY
CHRISTINA	LISA
COURTNEY	MEGAN
DANA	MELANIE
DANIELLE	MELISSA
DAWN	MICHELLE

MOLLY

NICOLE

RACHEL

SABRINA

SAMANTHA

SHANNON

STEPHANIE

TARA

TIFFANY

TRACY

VANESSA

WHITNEY

B O Y S

AARON

ADAM

ALEX

ALEXANDER

ASHLEY

BEN

BENJAMIN

BLAKE

BRADLEY

BRANDON

BRENDAN

BRETT

BRIAN

CASEY

DARRYL

DUSTIN

DYLAN

ERIC

ETHAN

IAN

JACOB

JAKE

JAMIE

JASON

JESSE

JONATHAN

JORDAN

JOSHUA

JUSTIN

LOREN

LUKE

MATTHEW

MAX

NICHOLAS

RYAN

SAM

SAMUEL

SCOTT

SEAN

TIMOTHY

TODD

ZACHARY

ZACK

FASHIONABLE CLASSICS

Fashionable classics are names that, while they happen to be trendy right now, nonetheless have staying power. If you give your child one of these fashionable classic names, you should know that he or she will be one of many with the same name. Nevertheless, these names won't necessarily brand him forever as a child of the eighties, the way their faddier cousins—Joshua, Jessica, et al—might.

Some of the following are among the most widely used names on the Nouveau Conservatif list; others figure prominently on most-popular lists around the country. What we consider fashionable classics for girls are:

ANNE
CAROLINE
ELIZABETH
EMILY
JANE
JULIA
KATE

KATHERINE (this is
    the fashionable
    spelling)
LAURA
LUCY
SARA(H)

For boys, the fashionable classics are:

ANDREW
CHARLES
CHRISTOPHER
DANIEL
EDWARD
HENRY
JAMES
JOHN

MATTHEW
MICHAEL (number
    one on current
    most popular lists)
PETER
STEPHEN
THOMAS
WILLIAM

BUT NICOLE IS MY FAVORITE NAME!

If all the foregoing has depressed you, if you've wanted to name your daughter Nicole since you were twelve years old and were not aware that thousands of other people had the same idea, we offer in apology a selection of names you might consider substituting for too-trendy favorites. What you consider an overused name or an acceptable substitute is to some extent a matter of personal style. Not all of the names on the "instead of" list have been pegged as so far in they're out, and some of the substitutes make a big leap forward in fashion. However, all of the possible substitute names bear some relationship to their overexposed counterparts in sound, feel, or taste, but their color is brighter and their texture a bit crisper.

G I R L S

Instead of:		Consider:
ALEXANDRA	----	ARABELLA
AL(L)ISON	----	ALICE
ALYSSA	----	ELIZA
AMANDA	----	MIRANDA
ASHLEY	----	AVERY
CAITLIN	----	KATHLEEN or BRONWEN
COURTNEY	----	CHELSEA or SYDNEY
DANA	----	DINAH

DANIELLE	----	LUCIENNE or SIMONE
EMILY	----	EMMA or EMILIA
ERIN	----	DEVON
HAYLEY/HALEY	----	LEILA or HIL(L)ARY
HEATHER	----	ROSEMARY or LILY
JENNIFER	----	JENNA
JESSICA	----	JESSA or JESSAMINE
JESSIE	----	JOSIE
JORDAN	----	GEORGIA
KELLY	----	KELSEY or QUINN
KIMBERLY	----	KIRBY or CHLOE
KRISTIN	----	KRISTA/CHRISTA
LAUREN	----	LAUREL
LINDSAY/LINDSEY	----	LACEY
LISA	----	LIZA or LUCY
MEGAN	----	REGAN or MARGARET
MELISSA	----	PRISCILLA or LARISSA

MOLLY	----	POLLY or DAISY
NICOLE	----	NICOLA
RACHEL	----	LEAH or RAYNA (Yiddish form of Catherine)
SAMANTHA	----	SUSANNAH or SOPHIA
SARA(H)	----	HANNAH
SHANNON	----	SHEA
TARA	----	NORA
TIFFANY	----	TESSA
TRACY	----	GRACE
VANESSA	----	VIOLET or CASSANDRA

B O Y S

Instead of:	----	Consider:
AARON	----	ABNER or EZRA
ADAM	----	AIDAN
ALEX	----	ALEC
BRANDON	----	BRAM
BRETT	----	BRICE
BRIAN	----	BRENNAN
CASEY	----	CLAY or CLANCY

CHRISTOPHER	----	CHRISTIAN
DYLAN	----	DUNCAN
ERIC	----	EMMETT
GARY	----	GRAY
JACOB	----	CALEB
JAKE	----	ABE or JACK
JASON	----	JASPER
JEREMY	----	JEREMIAH
JONATHAN	----	JONAS or JOHN
JORDAN	----	GEORGE
JOSHUA	----	JOSIAH
JUSTIN	----	JULIAN
KEVIN	----	CALVIN
MATTHEW	----	MATTHIAS
MAX	----	HARRY
NICHOLAS	----	TREVOR or COLIN
RYAN	----	RILEY
SAM	----	GUS or SIMM
SAMUEL	----	SAMSON
SEAN	----	SHAW
ZACHARY	----	ZACHARIAH
ZACK	----	ZEKE

So far out they're
On their way in

As the good ships Jennifer and Jason, Adam and Amy sail slowly out to sea for a well-deserved respite, what new fleet of names will begin to drift in? We foresee certain trends continuing, certain substitutions taking place, other old sources being tapped, different historical periods coming up for reconsideration.

Heaven knows the babies of today and tomorrow are entering a difficult and dangerous world, and there are two polar approaches you can take to meet this reality: arm or disarm. In the armed camp is a battalion of no-nonsense, no-nickname, responsible, bankable, grown-up citizen names. On the other side are the jaunty names: a raft of casual, happy-go-lucky, nothing-dire-can-befall-someone-with-such-a-cheery-name names.

Following is our selection of pick-hit names from both camps. These are names for the nineties and beyond, names that have style but aren't trendy, that sound new but not invented, that are solid but not blah.

THE O-NAMES

Friendliest of the whole crop of names that are so far out they're in are the names—primarily for boys—that end with the letter O. They almost seem to grin and call out a disarming "Hello!" We've already heard of a few trend-setting tykes with o-ending nicknames: a Benjamin who's called Benno and a Charles who was immediately dubbed Carlo. Some o-named grown-ups already in the mainstream are Emilio Estevez, Marlo Thomas, and Benno Schmidt, president of Yale University; also having an influence is Theo, the teenaged Cosby Show character.

Despite their breeziness, these names are not lightweight. The final *o* connotes a measure of strength we don't find in other vowel-ending names, such as Jessa or Jody.

There are a few good o-names for girls: Cleo, Lilo, Margo, and Marlo. For boys, the most likely to succeed of these spirited ulti-mate-o names are:

ALDO	LEO
ALONZO	LORENZO
ARLO	MARCO
ARNO	MILO
BENNO	NICO
BRUNO	ORLANDO
COSMO	OTTO
ELMO	PHILO
EMILIO	ROCCO
HORATIO	ROLLO
HUGO	THEO
JETHRO	WALDO

Viva Leo!

His real name was Leonard, Len. He'd changed it when he came East. "Len," he said. "A turd of a name. Who wants it? I mean, a name that ends in a nasalization, for Christ's sake. Leo, now. It's like Anna. They go on forever. You can *live* with a name like that."

—Sue Miller, *The Good Mother*, Harper & Row, 1986

THE RAF PILOT NAMES

Sharing an air of jaunty confidence with the O-names is a group of white-silk-scarved RAF Pilot names not yet in wide use in this country but poised for an imminent landing. They're on the cutting edge of fashion, combining the style of upper-crust England with the élan of the leather bomber jacket. We'd put them in the armed camp if they weren't so charming: You just know they will land their planes in time for tea. Fight the urge to give your son a little cowboy name and consider instead:

ADRIAN	JULIAN
ALISTAIR	MALCOLM
CLIVE	MILES
COLIN	NIGEL
DEREK	NOEL
DESMOND	REX
DUNCAN	ROBIN
GRAHAM	RUPERT
GUY	TREVOR
IVOR	

Nigel happens to be one of the names I've been crusading for as part of a plan to further Anglo-American friendship. I've always thought that one reason the English resent Americans is that we've never been able to favor the boys' names they favor, and they've always suspected us of thinking that their names are for sissies. Now here's my plan: For the next few years, a lot of Americans name their boys Nigel and Cecil and Cyril and Trevor and Simon, and we invite the English to name their boys American names. . . . Then, sooner or later, the United States will have a lot of grown-up men with English-sounding names and there will be a lot of people in England named LeRoy and Sonny and Bubba.

—Calvin Trillin, *Newsday,* July 22, 1987

THE IRISH SURNAME NAMES

From the days of "Sweet Rosie O'Grady" and "I'll Take You Home Again, Kathleen," Irish names have been consistently popular in this country. In the seventies and early eighties, Erin and Kelly and Shannon were among the top fifty names for girls, while Brian, Ryan, and Sean were equally popular boys' names.

Now, for the first time, we see an invasion of Irish surnames-as-first-names approaching. Three brothers on a current soap opera are named Cagney, Hogan, and Quinn, and television's most popular female cops are known by their last names, Cagney and Lacey. Ryan O'Neal and Farrah Fawcett gave their son the name Redmond. (In *Barry Lyndon,* O'Neal's character was named Redmond Barry.)

Most of these names work as well for girls as for boys. If this kind of name appeals to you, tap your own Irish roots for a family name, or look to this list:

BLAINE
BOWIE
BRADY
BRENNAN
CAGNEY
CALHOUN
CALLAHAN
CASSIDY
CLANCY
CULLEN
DEVLIN
DOLAN
DONOVAN
EGAN
FALLON
FARRELL
FINN
FLANAGAN
FLANNERY
FLYNN
GRADY
GRIFFIN
HOGAN
KANE

KEENAN
KENYON
KILLIAN
LACEY
LAUGHLIN
MAGEE
MAGILL
NOLAN
PHELAN
QUINLAN
QUINN
REDMOND
REGAN
RILEY
SHAW
SHEA
SHERIDAN
SWEENEY
TIERNEY
TULLY
WARD
WHALEN
WILEY/WYLIE

PLACE NAMES

Another group of names in the forefront of fashion not only connote a place, as most strongly ethnic names do, but actually denote
one. A few of these place names (Austin, Dallas, Denver, and Madi-
son) are more often used for boys, others (Devon, Macon, Nevada,
Portland, Sierra, Tulsa) are ambisexual, but the majority are or are
becoming exclusively female. Whatever their gender identification,
these names carry with them a real physical weight. Although some
of them may sound slightly outré right now, we predict we'll be
seeing more girls named:

ASIA	GENEVA
CAROLINA	GEORGIA
CATALINA	HOLLAND
CHELSEA	INDIA
CHINA	INDIANA
EDEN	JAMAICA
ELBA	ODESSA
FLORIDA	SAVANNAH
FRANCE	VENICE

GIRLS' NAMES: SASSY . . .

Another cheery group we see as due for a revival is the wisecracking
waitress/smart-aleck showgirl contingent, not recently seen or heard
from except on the late, late show in movies with titles like *Maisie
Was a Lady* and *Cain and Mabel,* made in the days when diners were
diners and McDonald's was still a farm. Leading the way for this
gum-snapping rejuvenation are little Mamie (Mary Willa) Gummer

(daughter of Meryl Streep), Stella McCartney (Paul and Linda's daughter), and Fifi Trixiebelle Geldof (child of Live Aid organizer Bob Geldof). While we draw the line at Toots and Queenie, we do foresee a bevy of little babes called:

BELLE	MAISIE
DIXIE	MAMIE
DORA	MILLIE
FIFI	MITZI
FRITZI	PATSY
JOSIE	PEG
KITTY	ROSIE
LOLA	ROXY
LULU	STELLA
MABEL	TESS
MAE	TRIXIE
MAGGIE	WINNIE

. . . AND SWEET

Continuing in the fragrant wake of such So Far In They're Out favorites as Jessica, Melissa, and Amanda, but with an offbeat charm that could make them the good-girl cousins of Fifi and Josie, are the delicate floral names, last popular at the turn of the century. Due for a revival are:

CAMELIA	FLORA
CLOVER	IVY
DAHLIA	JASMINE
DAISY	LAUREL

LILY   POSEY
MAGNOLIA   ROSE
MARIGOLD   VIOLET
ORCHID   ZINNIA
POPPY

As well as a few jewel-inspired names:

AMBER
BERYL
CORAL
JADE
RUBY

The names in the next group go beyond sweet and innocent to virtuous. These are the Puritan "virtue names," out of fashion for at least a century and a half but poised for rejuvenation along with Shaker simplicity and a feel for the classics and tradition. We're not suggesting anything as extreme as the Pilgrim names made up of entire Biblical verses, such as I-Walk-in-the-Valley-of-the-Shadow-of-Death Smith, but perhaps the time has come for such unadorned statements as, "I want a child who will be the living incarnation of this attribute."

AMITY   GRACE
CHARITY   HONOR
COMFORT   HOPE
CONSTANCE   MODESTY
FAITH   PATIENCE
FELICITY   PRUDENCE
FORTUNE   VERITY

REJUVENATED TRADITIONS

It seems as if America is at last ready to rediscover names rooted in the antebellum South—those used for blacks as well as for whites. A hundred years late, we're finally abolishing the taboo on slave names. In England, where there is no such shameful history to "forget," names like Dinah and Jemima are fashionably bestowed upon young ladies. These beautiful names—some Biblical in origin, some classical—deserve to be liberated and channeled back into the mainstream in this country as well. Overdue for recognition are:

G I R L S

BETHIA	ELIZA
CLEMENTINE	JEMIMA
CLEO	KEZIA(H)
DELIA	LETHIA
DELILAH	ODELIA
DINAH	SUKEY
DULCY	

B O Y S

AMOS	LUCIUS
CATO	OCTAVIUS
ELIJAH	RUFUS

Ashley, Brett, Melanie, and even Tara have already been released, but there is another set of names ready to leave the plantation for America at large, some of which have been tied to its moss-covered image for too long:

G I R L S

AN(N)ABEL(LE)
ARABELLA
SCARLETT
SUSANNAH

B O Y S

ASH
BEAU
CAMERON
CLAY
CLAYTON
CLEMENT
DAVIS
GRAY

BABY MEN AND WOMEN

It's time to get serious. This next group of names combines the brisk efficiency of the Androgynous Executives, the traditional values of the Nouveau Conservatifs, and the unadorned simplicity of the Grandma and Grandpa names. These names aren't cute or cuddly, sensitive or vulnerable, frivolous or fashionable . . . quite yet. They are the names of the rich great-aunts and uncles who, ten years ago, you might have prayed would not ask you to name your child after them. These names definitely fall in with the armed camp: They're ready to withstand any adult battle that awaits them. So be prepared for an army of gray-flannel-diapered babies named:

GIRLS

ADELINE	HELENA
AGATHA	HENRIETTA
AGNES	IMOGEN(E)
ALMA	JOSEPHINE
BEATRICE	KAY
BLANCHE	LETITIA
CLARA	MADEL(E)INE
CORA	MARIE
CORDELIA	MATILDA
CORNELIA	MAUD(E)
DOROTHEA	MERLE
ELEANOR	MINERVA
ELLA	NATALIE
EUDORA	NORA
EUGENIA	OLIVE
EVE	ROSALIND
FAY	RUTH
FRANCES	SYBIL
GWENDOLYN	SYLVIA
HARRIET	VIRGINIA
HAZEL	WILLA
HELEN	

BOYS

AMBROSE	BASIL
AMORY	BORIS
ARCHIBALD	CHESTER
AUGUSTINE	CLIFFORD

CLYDE	HECTOR
CONRAD	HIRAM
CORNELIUS	HOMER
CYRIL	HUGH
EDMOND	HUMPHREY
FELIX	ISIDORE
FLOYD	JOSEPH
FRANK	LIONEL
FREDERICK	LLOYD
GEORGE	OSCAR
GILES	PAUL
GODFREY	RALPH
GUS	SYLVESTER
GUY	WINSTON
HAL	WOODROW
HARRY	

COLD CASH NAMES

Most serious of all are the money names: Androgynous Executive names that not only hint at money but come right out and say it. You can't help but sound rich (we're only half joking) with a name like:

BARCLAY	GAYNOR
CASH	GRANT
CHASE	MERCEDES
FORBES	MORGAN
FORTUNE	PRICE
GAINES	PROSPER

STERLING   WORTH
TIFFANY

ALSO NOTED

There are some names we couldn't quite squeeze into any of the above categories, but are nonetheless worthy of a fresh look. So here we submit for reconsideration a list we freely admit is subjective, eclectic, and eccentric:

G I R L S

ARAMINTA	JULIET
BERNADETTE	LIBBY
CANDIDA	MIRANDA
CASSANDRA	OLIVIA
CELIA	PHOEBE
DIANTHA	PRISCILLA
ESME	QUINTINA
GENEVIEVE	SOPHIA
ISABEL	SYDNEY

B O Y S

ABEL	BYRON
ABNER	CALEB
ANGUS	CALVIN
ASA	CASPER
AXEL	CRISPIN

DEXTER	JASPER
ELI	LEVI
ELISHA	LUTHER
EMMETT	MOSES
EPHRAIM	NED
ESAU	SILAS
EZEKIEL	THADDEUS
EZRA	TITUS
FERGUS	TRISTAN
ISAAC	VIRGIL
JARVIS	ZELIG

So far out they'll Probably always be out

There are some names that are just too loaded with frumpy, dowdy, or nerdy baggage to come back into style now . . . or maybe ever. It usually takes three generations for a name to shed its moldy skin, and some of the names that follow have missed their chance. Others, popular just two generations back, may regenerate by the time our children have children. Right now, however, it's hard to imagine these names ever sounding fresh or cute or baby-appropriate again. On the other hand, if anyone had told us when we were growing up that Max and Jake would be among the trendy names of the eighties, we would have laughed them off the block.

GIRLS

AUGUSTA	BERTHA
BELVA	BEVERLY
BERNICE	DOLORES

DORIS
EDNA
ELSA
ENID
ESTELLE
ESTHER
ETHEL
EUNICE
FLORENCE
FRIEDA
GERTRUDE
GLADYS
GOLDA
HESTER
HORTENSE
IDA
IRENE
IRMA
JOYCE
LAVERNE
LENORE
LOIS
LORETTA
LORRAINE
LUCILLE

MADGE
MILDRED
MURIEL
MYRA
MYRNA
NORMA
OLGA
PAULA
PEARL
PHYLLIS
RHODA
RHONDA
ROBERTA
SELMA
SHIRLEY
THELMA
TRUDY
VELMA
VERA
VERNA
WANDA
WILHELMINA
YOLANDA
ZELDA

BOYS

ADOLPH
ALVIN
ARNOLD

BERNARD
BERTRAM
BURTON

CLARENCE
DEWEY
DONALD
DWAYNE
DWIGHT
EARL
EDGAR
EDWIN
EGBERT
ELMER
ELROY
ERNEST
EUGENE
FRANKLIN
GOMER
HAROLD
HARVEY
HERBERT
HERMAN
HUBERT
HYMAN
IRVING
IRWIN
JULIUS
LEONARD
LESTER
MARSHALL
MARTIN
MARVIN

MAURICE
MELVIN
MERVYN
MILTON
MORTIMER
MORTON
MURRAY
MYRON
NORMAN
ORVILLE
OSBERT
OSWALD
PERCY
RANDOLPH
RAYMOND
RONALD
RUDOLPH
SEYMOUR
SHELDON
SHERMAN
STANLEY
VERNON
VICTOR
VINCENT
WARREN
WILBUR
WILFRED
WILLARD
WOLFGANG

In Defense of Herbs

I think it is disgusting to stereotype every man named Herb as a nerd. This is exactly what the Burger King commercials are doing. I happen to know at least half a dozen men named Herb who are well liked, highly respectable, professional and successful businessmen. While I know that everyone named Herb cannot sue Burger King for their smear campaign, I do know that I can personally boycott the restaurant and petition all of my family and friends to do the same.

> —Christine M. Propheter, Sterling, Illinois (letter in
> *People* magazine, March 17, 1986)

What the rest of
The world is doing

Style may in many ways be personal, but it's never isolated: A name's fashion status can be judged only in relation to society in general. That's why we take a look here at what the rest of the world is doing about names. You'll find lists of the most popular boys' and girls' names in the United States. You'll see what the rich, famous, and royal—often the trend-setters in all manner of style—are naming their children. And you'll get an insight into how famous names, both real and fictional, have inspired naming trends or else taken a name forever off the general market.

THE TWENTY-FIVE MOST POPULAR GIRLS' AND BOYS' NAMES IN THE UNITED STATES

It's tough to get a truly accurate tally of which names are most popular in the United States: The federal government doesn't keep any statistics; neither do national agencies like the Census Bureau, or many state governments. In fact, we were about to fling up our hands in frustration when we stumbled upon Fred Krantz, a research analyst for the state of Wisconsin with a special interest in naming trends, who generously pointed us to five states that do keep accurate records on how many babies receive which names each year: New York, California, Tennessee, Oregon, and Wisconsin. With statistics from those five divergent places, we've compiled the following list of the twenty-five most popular names in the United States for 1986. A name's standing on the list includes all its variant spellings—Sarah and Sara considered together, for instance, make it the fifth most chosen girl's name.

G I R L S

1. JESSICA
2. AMANDA
3. ASHLEY
4. JENNIFER
5. SARA(H)
6. NICOLE
7. MEGAN
8. STEPHANIE
9. ELIZABETH
10. HEATHER
11. MELISSA
12. BRITTANY
13. AMBER
14. RACHEL
15. CHRISTINE/A
16. LAUREN
17. KATHERINE
18. DANIELLE
19. AMY
20. TIFFANY
21. EMILY
22. MICHELLE
23. KIMBERLY
24. SAMANTHA
25. CRYSTAL

B O Y S

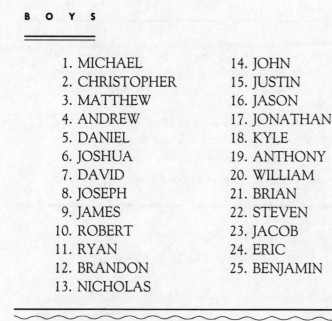

1. MICHAEL
2. CHRISTOPHER
3. MATTHEW
4. ANDREW
5. DANIEL
6. JOSHUA
7. DAVID
8. JOSEPH
9. JAMES
10. ROBERT
11. RYAN
12. BRANDON
13. NICHOLAS
14. JOHN
15. JUSTIN
16. JASON
17. JONATHAN
18. KYLE
19. ANTHONY
20. WILLIAM
21. BRIAN
22. STEVEN
23. JACOB
24. ERIC
25. BENJAMIN

Happy Birthday, Jennifer

I know it must be startling to realize how common your name must be for this greeting card to have been printed, but just think how much more disconcerting it would be if it also mentioned your remarkable sense of style, your love of Baroque music, your impatience with bureaucracy, and your conviction that your thighs should be thinner.

Enjoy your white wine and chocolate cake!

—Message on greeting card, Cards by Boynton

> Well, the current list of favorite names for babies is out, and it's interesting to note that in the year 2057, nursing homes will be inhabited by the likes of Nicole, Megan, Lauren, Jason, Ryan, and Lindsay.
>
> It will seem weird having a retired handyman named Ashley, a nun named Freedom and a doctor with the first name of Amiracle, but those are the current choices.
>
> —Erma Bombeck, Los Angeles *Times* Syndicate, July 1986

WHAT A DIFFERENCE A STATE MAKES

Why is Adam the ninth most popular boy's name in Wisconsin, and not even in the top twenty in New York, California, Oregon, or Tennessee? And what makes Stephanie a hit in California but a flop in New York?

While the standing of many popular names remains consistent from state to state, there are some wide variations.

In Tennessee, for instance, Brittany is the number-five girl's name, but isn't in the top ten of any other state we surveyed. Conversely, Tennesseeans shun Nicole, a top-ten hit in our other four states. For boys, parents in Tennessee love the name William, number seven on the list there but not a popularity leader anywhere else.

New Yorkers, on the other hand, favor Brian for boys and Christine, Danielle, and Crystal for girls far more than parents elsewhere. And parents in the more pastoral states of Wisconsin and Oregon like the names Amy, Heather, Megan, Kyle, and Brandon much better than do their counterparts in New York and California.

Style and ethnic differences account for many of the state-to-state variations in popularity lists. What does this mean for you? In general, if you want either a widely used or an unusual name, be ruled more by local than national popularity of names. Some cities and states keep their own tallies of most popular names and the results are usually published in the newspaper. Other methods for gauging a name's local popularity are to find out what people in your area are naming their babies by asking your obstetrician or prospective pediatrician, making friends with neighbors who have kids in nursery school (and who often have a firm handle on naming trends), and loitering in your neighborhood playground. And if you live in Wisconsin and name your daughter Crystal to be different, don't move to New York.

The longings of some Oregon parents were apparent in some of the names—Sunshine, June, July, April. Others seemed more realistic—Winter, Stormy, Rainsong.

. . . Parents left Oregon hospitals with Sterling, a Porsche, a Diamond, Ivory, Jade, a Sable, a Sheik, and . . . a Secret.

Romance in 1986 seemed to be one-sided. There were 16 Tristans, but alas, no Isolde; 183 Adams but no Eve; one Romeo and not a Juliet in sight; one Samson but no Delilah!

We couldn't help but wonder if at some future time, marriage certificates will show that Orlando has joined with Mississippi, that Colt has found his Bambi; Odysseus his Andromeda; Sarge his Liberty; Rock his Gem; Sheik his Dynasty; Royal his Roy'l; Serenity her Rowdy; Sky her Storm; Sparrow her Talon; and Sony the right Channel.

—From the section on names by state registrar Joseph D. Carney in the April 1987 *Oregon Health Trends*

It's a fact. Names come "in" and go "out" again. The Johns and Marys, Barbaras and Georges, Dorothys and Charleses have enjoyed a good run. We liked them so much, we used to give our dogs human names like Harry, Kate, and Jack. I suppose now we can expect to hear, "Come on in, Brandon, I'm getting cold." "Heel, Jessica." "Stay, Melissa." "Don't drink out of the toilet, Jonathan."

—Erma Bombeck, Los Angeles *Times* Syndicate, July 1986

STAR BABIES

Their births are announced on the six o'clock news, their pictures soon appear in magazines, and their names stand a chance of being in the papers for the rest of their lives.

They are the children of celebrities, and the names their famous parents choose for them are the essence of style. Mom and dad live in a sophisticated, glamorous environment where being fashionable—in everything down to your child's name—is de rigueur. And if the stars aren't following fashion, they are initiating it: Unusual names can become stylish after they're chosen by even a single superstar for his or her child. Cybill Shepherd's use of Clementine, for example, put an instant gloss on that old miner's daughter name.

Given that, it's not surprising that the following list reads like an amalgam of the So-Far-Out-They're-In and the So-Far-In-They're-Out groups. Since most celebrities don't mind being noticed, many of them pick attention-grabbing names for their offspring (with the knowledge, too, that the other kids in their children's circle will take these names for granted). The few exceptions are often family names—Paul McCartney's Mary and Richard Thomas's Barbara, for example, are named for their grandmothers.

For the most part, we included only children born in the last decade to well-known celebrities, bending the rules when the names were exceptional and/or the parents were superstars: Chastity, daughter of Sonny and Cher, is one such example. Middle names appear when they were accessible. Also, we realize that none of these children arrived without both a mother and a father, and offer our apologies to those lesser-known parents who might not have received billing here.

Star baby names

AISHA	____	Stevie Wonder
ALEX	____	William Hurt
ALEX	____	Lindsay Wagner
ALEXA RAY	____	Christie Brinkley and Billy Joel
ALEXANDER	____	Melanie Griffith
ALEXANDRA (SASHA)	____	Jessica Lange and Mikhail Baryshnikov
ALEXANDRA	____	Christopher Reeve

ALEXANDRA BEATRIS	- - - -	Tyne Daly and Georg Stanford Brown
ALEXANDRIA	- - - -	Keith Richards and Patti Hanson
ALEXIS	- - - -	Ted Danson
ANDREAS (boy)	- - - -	Susan Lucci
ANNA KATE	- - - -	John Denver
ANNABEL	- - - -	Lynn Redgrave
ANNIE	- - - -	Kevin Costner
ARNE ROSS	- - - -	Diana Ross
ASHLEY STEVEN	- - - -	George Hamilton and Alana Hamilton Stewart
AUBREE (girl)	- - - -	Jimmy Connors
AUSTIN DEVEREUX (boy)	- - - -	Michelle Phillips
BARBARA (triplet)	- - - -	Richard Thomas
BARTHOLOMEW	- - - -	Timothy Bottoms
BEN	- - - -	Jeff Daniels

BENJAMIN	----	Raul Julia
BENJAMIN SIMON	----	Carly Simon and James Taylor
BOSTON (boy)	----	Season Hubley and Kurt Russell
BRAWLEY KING	----	Nick Nolte
BRETT DAVID	----	Jimmy Connors
BRIGITTE MICHAEL	----	Sting
CADE RICHMOND (boy)	----	Keith Carradine
CAITLIN	----	Shaun Cassidy
CALEY (girl)	----	Chevy Chase
CALICO	----	Alice Cooper
CAMERON MORRELL (boy)	----	Michael Douglas
CARLY	----	John Ritter
CASEY (girl)	----	Kris Kristofferson and Rita Coolidge

CASSANDRA	----	Charlie Sheen
CHARLI (girl)	----	Melba Moore
CHARLIE	----	Susan St. James and Dick Ebersole
CHASTITY	----	Sonny and Cher
CHERISH	----	Charlene Tilton
CHLOE	----	Candice Bergen and Louis Malle
CHLOE ROSE	----	Olivia Newton-John
CHRISTIAN (twin)	----	Mel Gibson
CHRISTOPHER	----	Kenny Rogers
CHRISTOPHER	----	Pia Zadora and Meshulem Riklis
CHUDNEY LANE	----	Diana Ross
CLEMENTINE	----	Cybill Shepherd
CODY (boy)	----	Kenny Loggins
CONDOLA PHYLEA	----	Phylicia and Ahmad Rashad

CONOR	----	Eric Clapton
CROSBY (boy)	----	Kenny Loggins
CYDNEY CATHALENE	----	Chevy Chase
CYRUS ZACHARIAH (twin)	----	Cybill Shepherd
DAISY	----	Mia Farrow and André Previn
DASHIELL	----	Harry Anderson
DIMITRI	----	Ursula Andress and Harry Hamlin
DORIAN HENRY	----	Lindsay Wagner
DREE LOUISE	----	Mariel Hemingway
DUSTIN (girl, twin)	----	Debby Boone
DYLAN (girl)	----	Mia Farrow
EDWARD (twin)	----	Mel Gibson
ELETTRA	----	Isabella Rossellini
ELIJAH BLUE	----	Cher and Gregg Allman

ELIZABETH SCARLETT	----	Mick Jagger and Jerry Hall
ELVIS BROOKE	----	Tony Perkins and Berry Berenson
EMANUEL NOAH	----	Debra Winger and Timothy Hutton
ETHAN	----	Jackson Browne
EVA MARIA LIVIA	----	Susan Sarandon
FIFI TRIXIEBELLE FLEETWOOD STARR	---- ----	Bob Geldof Tom Robbins
FLETCHER	----	Mia Farrow and André Previn
GABRIELLE (twin) GASTON GIGI SOON YI	---- ---- ----	Debby Boone Jaclyn Smith Mia Farrow and André Previn
GILLIAN CATHERINE	----	Patty Hearst
GRACE	----	Rhea Perlman and Danny DeVito

GRACE JANE	----	Meryl Streep
GWYNETH (triplet)	----	Richard Thomas
HANNAH	----	Mel Gibson
HANNAH JANE	----	Jessica Lange and Sam Shepard
HARMONY (boy)	----	Susan St. James
HARPER (boy)	----	Paul Simon
HAYLEY ROSE	----	Jeff Bridges
HENRY	----	Meryl Streep
HOMER	----	Bill Murray
INDIA SERENE	----	Philip Michael Thomas and Sheila DeWindt
ISAAC	----	Mandy Patinkin
ISABELLE	----	Jeff Bridges
JACOB	----	Dustin Hoffman
JACOB	----	Rhea Perlman and Danny DeVito
JACOB WALKER	----	Nora Ephron and Carl Bernstein

JADE	----	Mick Jagger and Bianca Jagger
JAKE	----	Sting
JAKE	----	Blythe Danner
JAMES LEROY AUGUSTIN	----	Mick Jagger and Jerry Hall
JAMES LOUIS	----	Paul and Linda McCartney
JAMIE (girl)	----	Joan Lunden
JAMIE (boy)	----	Kim Alexis
JASON	----	John Ritter
JAZMIN	----	Julius "Dr. J" Irving
JENNIFER	----	Billy Crystal
JESSE	----	Don Johnson and Patti D'Arbanville
JESSICA	----	Jeff Bridges
JESSICA GRACE	----	Joe Namath
JOCELYN (twin)	----	Ron Howard
JOE	----	Sting
JORDAN ALEXANDER	----	Debby Boone
JORDAN ELIZABETH	----	Cheryl Ladd
JULIANA	----	Shelley Long

KADY	----	Pia Zadora and Meshulem Riklis
KATE	----	Sting
KATE	----	Ted Danson
KATE	----	Meredith Baxter-Birney and David Birney
KATE GARRY	----	Goldie Hawn and Bill Hudson
KATHARINE JANE (KATIE)	----	Jane Seymour
KATHERINE	----	Martin Short
KEITA	----	Stevie Wonder
KEVIN JOHN	----	Tatum O'Neal and John McEnroe
KIMBERLY	----	Rod Stewart and Alana Hamilton Stewart
LARK SONG	----	Mia Farrow and André Previn
LEE DAVIS	----	Bruce Boxleitner
LEIGH	----	Susan Lucci
LIAM	----	Faye Dunaway and Terry O'Neill

LILY	----	Jill Clayburgh and David Rabe
LILY	----	Mary Steenburgen and Malcolm McDowell
LILY	----	Kevin Costner
LINDSAY (girl)	----	Billy Crystal
LINDSAY (girl)	----	Joan Lunden
LOLA	----	Julian Schnabel
LORCAN (boy)	----	Peter O'Toole
LUCIE	----	Rhea Perlman and Danny DeVito
LYDIA MARIE	----	Patty Hearst
LYRIC (girl)	----	Robby Benson and Karla DeVito
MABLE ELLEN	----	Tracey Ullman
MALCOLM	----	Harrison Ford and Melissa Mathison
MARY	----	Paul and Linda McCartney
MARY WILLA	----	Meryl Streep
MATTHEW	----	Christopher Reeve

MATTHEW PHINEAS (twin)	----	Mia Farrow and André Previn
MAX	----	Dustin Hoffman
MAX	----	Henry Winkler
MAX	----	Jill Eikenberry and Michael Tucker
MAX EPHRON	----	Nora Ephron and Carl Bernstein
MAX SAMUEL	----	Amy Irving and Steven Spielberg
MELODY	----	Philip Michael Thomas and Sheila DeWindt
MIMI	----	Donna Summer
MOLLIE (twin)	----	Meredith Baxter-Birney and David Birney
MOLLY	----	Mary Beth Hurt and Paul Schrader

MOLLY ARIEL (twin)	- - - -	Cybill Shepherd
MOLLY MIRANDA	- - - -	Erica Jong
MOSES	- - - -	Mia Farrow
NATHAN	- - - -	Mark Hamill
NATHANIEL	- - - -	Barbara Mandrell
NAVARONE ANTHONY	- - - -	Priscilla Presley
OLIVER	- - - -	Goldie Hawn and Bill Hudson
OLIVER	- - - -	Martin Short
OSGOOD ROBERT	- - - -	Tony Perkins and Berry Berenson
PAIGE (twin)	- - - -	Ron Howard
PALLAS (girl)	- - - -	Louise Erdrich and Michael Dorris
PERSIA (girl)	- - - -	Louise Erdrich and Michael Dorris
PETER (twin)	- - - -	Meredith Baxter-Birney and David Birney

PILAR (triplet)	- - - -	Richard Thomas
RACHEL	- - - -	Kathleen Turner
RACHEL (twin)	- - - -	Jane Pauley and Garry Trudeau
RAMONA	- - - -	Jonathan Demme
RAPHAEL EUGENE	- - - -	Robert DeNiro
RAUL SIGMUND	- - - -	Raul Julia
REBECCA	- - - -	Dustin Hoffman
REDMOND JAMES FAWCETT	- - - -	Farrah Fawcett and Ryan O'Neal
RHONDA SUZANNE	- - - -	Diana Ross
ROSIE	- - - -	Rachel Ward and Bryan Brown
ROSIE LEA	- - - -	Roger Daltrey
ROSS (twin)	- - - -	Jane Pauley and Garry Trudeau
RUBY	- - - -	Rod Stewart and Kelly Emberg

SAGE MOON BLOOD (boy)	----	Sylvester Stallone
SAM	----	Bruce Boxleitner
SAMANTHA	----	Sally Struthers
SARAH EMILY	----	Joan Lunden
SARAH MARIA	----	Carly Simon and James Taylor
SASCHA (twin, boy)	----	Mia Farrow and André Previn
SATCHEL	----	Mia Farrow and Woody Allen
SCHUYLER ELIZABETH	----	Sissy Spacek
SEAN	----	Rod Stewart and Alana Hamilton Stewart
SEAN TIMOTHY	----	Tatum O'Neal and John McEnroe
SEARGEOH (boy)	----	Sylvester Stallone
SOPHIE FREDERICA ALOHILANI	----	Bette Midler

SPENCER MARGARET	_ _ _ _	Jaclyn Smith
STARLITE MELODY	_ _ _ _	Marisa Berenson
STELLA	_ _ _ _	Paul and Linda McCartney
STELLA	_ _ _ _	Julian Schnabel
SUNSHINE (girl)	_ _ _ _	Susan St. James
SYDNEY BROOKE (girl)	_ _ _ _	O. J. Simpson
TESSA	_ _ _ _	Debby Boone
THEODORA DUPREE	_ _ _ _	Keith Richards and Patti Hanson
THOMAS	_ _ _ _	Jane Pauley and Garry Trudeau
TRACEE JOY	_ _ _ _	Diana Ross
VIVIAN	_ _ _ _	Debbie Allen
WILLA	_ _ _ _	Lindsay Crouse and David Mamet
WILLIAM	_ _ _ _	Susan St. James and Dick Ebersole
WILLIAM	_ _ _ _	Mel Gibson
WILLOW AMBER (girl)	_ _ _ _	Roger Daltrey

WYATT	- - - -	Goldie Hawn and Kurt Russell
ZACHARY	- - - -	Robin Williams
ZACHARY	- - - -	Gregory Hines
ZOE EMILY	- - - -	Henry Winkler

~~~~~~~~~~~~~~~~~~~~~~~~~~~~~

Naming According to Cosby

Always end the name of your child with a vowel, so that when you yell, the name will carry. I do not see how a mother can hang out of her window and do anything much with a cry of "Torvald!" A nervous mother needs an *o* or an *i* or an *e* because they last long enough to get the kid home for his beating. That mother also can't be heard by her other son, Dag, because the *g* sound doesn't stretch any better than the *d.*

If you must put consonants in your child's name, put them in the middle, where an *n* or two *s*'s or even four will work, as long as there's a vowel at the end. For example, if your child were named Winnou, you could linger on the "Winn" for a long time and then finish up strong with the "oooo." You could get past more than two sewers with that name: You could get a couple of blocks.

—Bill Cosby, *Fatherhood,* Doubleday & Co., 1986

(Cosby's own children are one boy, Ennis William, and four girls: Ensa Camille, Erika Ranee, Errin Charlene, and Evin Harrah.)

Frank Zappa's children:

MOON UNIT
DWEEZIL
AHMET EMUUKHA RODAN
DIVA

Much of the public believed when China [Slick, daughter of Grace] was born that her parents had named her "god." That was merely a Starship joke. As for her real name, China used to hate it. "But the more I've grown up, the more I've begun to like it. I think me and Moon and Dweezil and Chynna [Phillips, daughter of Michelle] are a lot more fortunate than people who got names like Mary or Sue or Ted."

Daily News Magazine, May 31, 1987

Bette Midler on naming her daughter Sophie: "We wanted something that would go with the European sound of my husband's name [Martin von Haselberg]. We went around Cornelia and Chloe and Zoe and all through the Brontes. We think Sophie sounds like an impoverished Austrian princess who is forced to marry a coarse member of the French bourgeoisie. He doesn't have quite her delicate upbringing, but he has piles of money. That's the story we made up for her."

—*People* magazine, January 5, 1987

ANDREW AND ANNE, ATTORNEYS-AT-LAW

Among the children of the partners of one prestigious New York law firm, several names appear more than once. In order of the number of occurrences, the names in favor with the rich and conservative include:

G I R L S

KATHERINE (5) ELIZA (2)
ELIZABETH (4) JENNIFER (2)
MARGARET (3) LESLIE (2)
ANNE (2)

B O Y S

JAMES (7) CHRISTOPHER (6)

ANDREW (5)   DAVID (4)
JOHN (5)   RICHARD (4)
WILLIAM (5)   DANIEL (3)
ALEXANDER (4)   PETER (3)

And two each of the following:

ANTHONY   LEE
BENJAMIN   MATTHEW
CHARLES   MICHAEL
GREGORY   ROBERT
JONATHAN   TIMOTHY

As proof that all is not sedate when law partners leave the office, we note the following names that break rank with the traditional pack. Included among the children of partners in the same firm are one each called:

G I R L S

———————

ANYA   LARA
CHAYA   LUANA
EVANGELINE   MARIANA
LANDIS   MOIRA

B O Y S

———————

AVROHOM   DONALDSON
CARROLL   DYLAN
CLAYTON   GARRICK
COLIN   GRAY

OGDEN   SHERWOOD
PARKER

WHAT THE ROYAL ARE NAMING THEIR CHILDREN, or NOBLESSE OBLIGE

For the most part, the British royal family and peerage have limited themselves to a prescribed pool of sanctioned names. They seem to use as many as possible for each child, a fact Lady Diana must have been all too aware of as she stumbled over the litany of her future husband's names during their wedding ceremony. When the Prince and Princess of Wales had their own sons, Tyrone—or even Trevor—were decidedly not open options. The results: Princes William Arthur Philip Louis and Henry Charles Albert David. Prince Charles's sister Anne went with the program when she named her first child Peter Mark Andrew, but proclaimed a measure of independence when she named her daughter Zara Anne Elizabeth. Some of the young royal cousins include Alexander Patrick Gregers Richard (Earl of Ulster), Lady Davina Elizabeth Alice Benedikte Windsor, Lady Rose Victoria Birgitte Louise Windsor, Lord Frederick Michael George David Louis Windsor, and Lady Gabriella (called Ella) Marisa Alexandra Ophelia Windsor.

Debrett's Peerage, the *Who's Who* of the British nobility, is brimming with the expected young Lady Victorias and Hon. Jameses; also popular among the present generation of junior aristocrats are:

G I R L S

ALEXANDRA   BEATRIX
ARABELLA   CAMILLA

CAROLINE	JANE
CHARLOTTE	JEMIMA
CLAIRE	JESSAMINE
CLEMENTINE	JULIA
DAPHNE	KATHERINE
ELIZABETH	LETITIA
EMMA	LOUISE
FIONA	NATALIA
FLORA	NICOLA
FRANCES	OLIVIA
FREDERICA	PHILIPPA
GEORGINA	ROSE
GILLIAN	ROSEMARY
GWYNETH	SARAH
HARRIET	SERENA
HENRIETTA	SOPHIE
IONA	SUSANNAH
ISABEL(LA)	

B O Y S

ALEXANDER	PATRICK
BENEDICT	PEREGRINE
CHRISTOPHER	PIERS
EDWARD	RICHARD
HUGH	RODERICK
IAN	THOMAS
JAMES	WILLIAM
JOHN	

This is not to say that British aristocracy is ready to surrender its reputation for eccentricity. Sprinkled among the Johns and Julias in *Debrett's* and *Burke's Peerage* are:

G I R L S

AGNETA	MARIGOLD
ALBINIA	MYEE
ARIADNE	NINO
ATALANTA	OOHAGH
BETTINE	PANDORA
COSIMA	PELLINE
DOUNE	PETREA
FENELLA	PRIMROSE
FILUMENA	RHIANNON
JENNET	SERAPHINA
JESSAMY	SIBYLLA
LAVENDER	TAMSIN
LENKA	VASHTI
MABELL	

B O Y S

ALARIC	HAMISH
DENZIL	LOEL
DICKON	MONTAGU
DREWETT	QUINTON
EUAN	VICARY

Also of note are the names of the children of Monaco's Princess Caroline: Andrea, a boy, his brother Pierre, and Charlotte Marie

Pomeline. According to unreliable media sources—but of interest here anyway—Caroline is in a "royal snit" because her father insists on calling her daughter "little Gracie."

THE SHIRLEY TEMPLE SYNDROME

In the early thirties, there was a sudden rise in popularity of the name Shirley, almost as meteoric as the fame of its dimpled inspiration, Shirley Temple, every mother's dream. Over the years, there have been other celebrities whose names (often not the ones they were born with) projected attractive enough images to appeal to lots of their fans when they became parents: Witness, for example, the legions of Debbies (after Reynolds), Judys (for Garland), and Garys (in honor of Cooper) born in our own generation. Unfortunately, these names can age and their popularity wane along with the celebrities who inspire them. The danger, then, of naming your child after a star is obvious: today's fashionable little Whitney or Brooke may be tomorrow's Shirley. Our list of celebrities who are influencing current naming trends would have to include:

AIDAN Quinn
ALI (b. Alice) MacGraw
ALLY Sheedy
BEAU (b. Lloyd Vernet) Bridges
BROOKE Shields
CANDICE Bergen
CARLY Simon
CHRISTIE Brinkley
DACK Rambo
DUSTIN Hoffman

Bob DYLAN (b. Zimmerman)
HAYLEY Mills
HARRISON Ford
IAN Fleming
JACQUELINE Kennedy
JESSICA Lange
JODIE Foster
JUSTINE Bateman
KIRK Cameron
LATOYA Jackson

LAUREN (b. Mary)
  Hutton
LINDSAY Wagner
LIZA Minnelli
MACKENZIE Phillips
MEREDITH
  Baxter-Birney
MIA (b. Maria)
  Farrow
MORGAN (b. Patsy)
  Fairchild

RYAN (b. Patrick
  Ryan) O'Neal
SAM Shepard
SAMANTHA (b.
  Victoria Louise)
  Eggar
SEAN (b. Thomas)
  Connery
SHAUN Cassidy
VANESSA Redgrave
WHITNEY Houston

Other names, such as DARYL Hannah and GLENN Close, while not being used much themselves, are having the indirect influence of making male names more popular for girls.

STAR-SANCTIONED NAMES

When Brooke Shields confided to us about her Calvins, we all knew who (and what) she was talking about. While Calvin Klein may have made his name famous, it's not linked to his persona with iron chains, the way names like Thelonius and Tennessee (see "There's Only One Aretha," page 000) are bound to their sole owners. What we're saying is that the star-sanctioned names that follow are all viable options: There's no reason you can't have a little Calvin (or Flannery or Paloma) of your own.

ARLO Guthrie
AVA Gardner
BETTE Davis/Midler

BIANCA Jagger
BLYTHE Danner
BO (b. Mary

Cathleen) Derek
BRONSON Pinchot
CALVIN Klein
CLORIS Leachman
CORETTA Scott-King
DASHIELL (b. Samuel
Dashiell) Hammett
DINAH (b. Frances)
Shore
EUDORA Welty
FARRAH (b. Mary
Farrah) Fawcett
FLANNERY
O'Connor
GILDA Radner
ISADORA Duncan
JACKSON Browne
JONI (b. Roberta
Joan) Mitchell
MARIEL Hemingway
(named for Cuban
bay where her
parents used to fish)
MARLO (b. Margaret
Julia) Thomas

MARLON Brando
MELBA (b. Beatrice)
Moore
MERCEDES (b.
Carlotta Mercedes)
McCambridge
MERYL (b. Mary
Louise) Streep
NASTASSJA Kinski
PALOMA Picasso
PIPER (b. Rosetta)
Laurie
QUINCY Jones
RAQUEL Welch
ROONE Arledge
RORY (b. Francis)
Calhoun
SHANA Alexander
SHEENA Easton
TALIA Shire
TATUM O'Neal
TEMPESTT Bledsoe
TYNE Daly
URSULA Andress

THERE'S ONLY ONE ARETHA

And only one Elton, Sigourney, Tuesday, and all the other names listed here. What we're trying to tell you is that there is not room in this world for two; these names are taken. Giving one to your child is like sentencing her to a lifetime of saying, for instance, "Yes, as in Sonny and . . ." These one-person names include:

ADLAI Stevenson
ADOLF (the classic case) Hitler
ANAIS Nin
ARETHA Franklin
ARSENIO Hall
AYN Rand
BURL (b. Icle) Ives
CHAKA Khan
CHARLTON Heston
CHASTITY Bono
CHER (b. Cherilyn) Bono Allman
CHEVY (b. Cornelius Charles) Chase
CLEAVON Little
CLEVELAND Amory
CONWAY (b. Harold) Twitty
CORNEL Wilde
DABNEY Coleman
DEMI Moore
DENZEL Washington
DESI (Desiderio) Arnaz (Sr. and Jr.)
EARTHA Kitt
EERO Saarinen
ELDRIDGE (b. Leroy Eldridge) Cleaver
ELTON (b. Reginald) John
ELVIS Presley
ENGELBERT (b. Arnold) Humperdinck
EVITA (b. Maria Estella) Peron
GORE (b. Eugene) Vidal
GOWER Champion
HEDDA Hopper
HERMIONE Gingold
HUME Cronyn
HUMPHREY Bogart
JESSAMYN West
JUDAS Iscariot
KEELY Smith
KIEFER Sutherland
LEVAR Burton
LEONTYNE (b. Mary) Price
LYNDON Johnson
MADONNA (Madonna Louise Ciccone)
MAHALIA Jackson
MARE Winningham

MCGEORGE Bundy

MCLEAN Stevenson

MERCE Cunningham

MERLIN Olsen

MONTGOMERY (b. Edward Montgomery) Clift

MOSS Hart

OPRAH Winfrey

ORAL Roberts

ORNETTE Coleman

ORSON Welles/Bean (okay, so there are two, but what do you remember about Orson Bean besides his name?)

PETULA Clark

REGIS Philbin

RING (b. Ringgold Wilmar) Lardner

ROCK (b. Roy) Hudson

RUDYARD Kipling

SADA Thompson

SADE

SARGENT (b. Robert Sargent) Shriver

SEASON Hubley

SHERWOOD Anderson

SIGOURNEY (b. Susan) Weaver

SOMERSET (b. William Somerset) Maugham

STOCKARD Channing

STROM (J. Strom) Thurmond

SWOOSIE Kurtz

TALLULAH Bankhead

TENNESSEE (b. Thomas) Williams

THELONIOUS Monk

THURGOOD Marshall

TREAT Williams

TRINI Lopez

TRUMAN Capote

TUESDAY (b. Susan) Weld

TWYLA Tharp

UTA Hagen

VANNA White

VIDAL Sassoon

WAYLON Jennings

WYNTON Marsalis

YUL (b. Taidje) Brynner

There have also been fictional characters whom we all see as the quintessence of some quality—usually either stark black or white—to the point where what they are called becomes more totem than name. Ebenezer, for example, will always represent a bah, humbug! mentality, Cinderella will eternally wear a glass slipper, and Kermit will be forever green.

Other cases in point:

L'il ABNER
ALVIN and the
  Chipmunks
BARBIE doll
CASPER the friendly
  ghost
CINDERELLA
CLARABELL the
  clown
CONAN the
  Barbarian
EBENEZER Scrooge
ELMER Fudd
ELSIE the cow
FELIX the cat
FERDINAND the bull
GARFIELD the cat
GOMER Pyle
GROVER on Sesame
  Street
HAMLET
HARVEY the rabbit

IAGO
ICHABOD Crane
JEM is outrageous
KERMIT the frog
LINUS
LOLITA
Little LULU
MAYNARD G. Krebs
MYRTLE the turtle
OLIVE Oyl
OPHELIA
OSCAR the grouch
POLLYANNA
RHETT Butler
RUDOLPH the
  red-nosed reindeer
SHERLOCK Holmes
SHIRA, princess of
  power
TINKERBELL
URIAH Heep
WINNIE the Pooh

NEU SPELLINGS

The creative spellings of these celebrities' names have, for better or worse, become accepted alternatives. If you're tempted to follow suit and spell your child's name in an original way, check the dangers in "Catherine, Katharine, and Kathrynne," page 197.

ANN-MARGRET
BARBRA Streisand
BETTE Davis (the ambiguity of this name led to two camps of followers: those who used the French, one-syllable pronunciation, and those who used it as a variant spelling of Betty)
CAROLE (b. Jane) Lombard (the final E was a publicity man's mistake, but it led to a rash of babies named Carole)
CYBILL Shepherd
CYNDI Lauper
DIAHANN (b. Carol Diahann) Carroll
DIONNE Warwick

DYAN (b. Samille Diane) Cannon
EFREM Zimbalist
ELAYNE Boosler
EVONNE Goolagong
FREDRIC (b. Ernest Frederick) March
GEENA Davis
JACKEE Harry
JACLYN Smith
JAYNE (b. Vera Jane) Mansfield
JERMAINE Jackson
JIMI (b. Johnny Allen) Hendrix
JONI (b. Roberta Joan) Mitchell
KHRYSTYNE Haye
MARGAUX Hemingway
PHYLICIA Rashad
STEFANIE (b. Stefania Zofia) Powers

ELECTRONIC INSPIRATION

There is little doubt that movies and television—TV in particular—
have had considerable influence on naming patterns. Sometimes the
effect has been immediate; often it becomes evident when the generation who watched certain popular shows as children and adoles-
cents reaches child-bearing age.

The Westerns and hillbilly shows that rode the airwaves in the
late fifties and through the sixties, for example, led to the hordes
of city cowboys in the playgrounds of the seventies, to wit:

ADAM	*Bonanza*
BARNABY	*Wagon Train*
BART	*Maverick*
BEAU	*Wells Fargo, Maverick*
BEN	*Bonanza*
BRENT	*Maverick*
BRET	*Maverick*
CHEYENNE	*Cheyenne*
FLINT	*Wagon Train*
JARROD	*Big Valley*
JASON	*Wanted: Dead or Alive, Here Come the Brides*
JEB	*Wells Fargo*
JED	*Rawhide, How the West Was Won*
JEREMY	*Here Come the Brides*
JOSH	*Wanted: Dead or Alive*
JOSHUA	*Here Come the Brides*
LUCAS	*Rifleman*
LUKE	*How the West Was Won*
MATT	*Gunsmoke*

SETH   *Wagon Train*
SIMON   *Rawhide*
ZEB   *How the West Was Won*

Noncowboy characters who have made (and in some cases are still making) an impact would have to include:

ADAM   *Dynasty, The Guiding Light,*
                            General Hospital, The
                            Edge of Night
ADDISON (surname   *Moonlighting*
but used as first)
ALEX   *Family Ties*
ALEXIS   *Dynasty*
ALLIE   *Kate & Allie*
ALLISON   *Peyton Place, Search for To-*
                            morrow
AMANDA   *Dynasty, Scarecrow and Mrs.*
                            King, Days of Our Lives
ANGELA   *Falcon Crest, Who's the Boss?*
ANGELICA   *Dallas*
ASHLEY (f)   *The Young and the Restless*
BARNABY   *Barnaby Jones*
BEAU   *As the World Turns*
BENJAMIN   *The Graduate*
BLAIR (f)   *The Facts of Life*
BLAKE (m)   *Dynasty*
BLISS   *The Colbys*
BRANDY   *The Edge of Night, The Guid-*
                            ing Light
BRITTANY   *Another World*

BROCK	*The Young and the Restless*
BROOKE	*All My Children, Days of Our Lives, General Hospital, The Bold and the Beautiful*
CAGNEY (surname but used as first)	*Cagney & Lacey*
CAIN	*Santa Barbara*
CAITLIN	*Airwolf*
CARESS	*Dynasty*
CHASE	*Falcon Crest, General Hospital*
CHRISSY	*Three's Company*
CLAIR	*The Cosby Show*
CLAY	*Search for Tomorrow, Edge of Night, Loving*
CODY	*Riptide*
COLE	*Falcon Crest*
CRICKET	*The Young and the Restless*
DARRIN	*Bewitched*
DELILAH	*One Life to Live*
DEX	*Dynasty*
DOMINIQUE	*Dynasty*
EMMA	*Kate & Allie*
ERICA	*All My Children*
FALLON (f)	*Dynasty*
FRISCO	*General Hospital*
GWYNETH	*Loving*
HARRY	*Night Court*
INDIA	*Somerset*
JAIME (f)	*The Bionic Woman*
JEFF	*77 Sunset Strip*

JENNA	*Dallas*
JENNIFER	*Hart to Hart, Family Ties*
JESSICA	*Murder, She Wrote*
JONATHAN	*Hart to Hart*
KATE	*Kate & Allie*
KAYLA	*Days of Our Lives*
KELLY (m)	*I Spy*
KELLY (f)	*Bachelor Father, Charlie's Angels*
KIMBERLY	*Diff'rent Strokes, Days of Our Lives*
KIRBY (f)	*Dynasty*
KRYSTLE	*Dynasty*
LACEY (surname used as first)	*Cagney & Lacey*
LUKE	*General Hospital*
MADELINE (Maddie)	*Moonlighting*
MALLORY	*Family Ties*
NICHOLAS	*Eight Is Enough*
PHOEBE	*All My Children*
RAVEN	*The Edge of Night*
SABRINA	*Charlie's Angels*
SAM	*McCloud, Cheers*
SAMANTHA	*Bewitched, My Sister Sam, Who's the Boss?*
SENECA (m)	*Ryan's Hope*
SIERRA	*As the World Turns*
SIMON	*The Saint*
SKYE (m)	*All My Children*
SLOANE (f)	*Capitol*
SOPHIA	*Santa Barbara*
TABITHA	*Bewitched*

TIFFANY	*Charlie's Angels*
VANESSA	*The Cosby Show*
WINTER (f)	*The Edge of Night*
ZANE	*Another World*
ZOE	*Somerset*

Soap Names

Often the same names—Jenny, Mark, Tony, Jason, Patty, Maggie, Amanda, and Kate—are given to characters on several soaps. . . . If something works on one soap (opera), there is no hesitation in adapting or blatantly copying it for another series. Names that are particularly descriptive of certain characters on a soap are used to continue that descriptive allusion on another one. Jennys, for example, appear to be women who are good and beautiful but often victimized between their triumphant moments.

—Seli Groves, *Soaps,* Contemporary Books, 1983

In March 1987, CBS introduced a new soap opera called "The Bold and the Beautiful." Among the leading male characters were a Ridge, a Thorn, and a Storm. Said John J. O'Connor in his *New York Times* review: "If nothing else, the names concocted for their characters are alone worth dipping into 'The Bold and the Beautiful' for a hoot or two."

IMAGE

As his name is, so is he.

—Samuel, XXV, 25

Every name sends out signals even before it's attached to a specific physical presence. It transmits subliminal messages and reverberations of its own: a level of energy, an intensity of color and sheen, a texture.

The image of the name you choose will precede your child throughout his or her lifetime. Strangers will use it as the basis for making certain assumptions about him or her: as someone intellectual or physical, attractive or plain, well-born or plebeian, unique or one of the crowd. Of course, your child's personality and presence will be the real determining factors in other people's judgments, but the power of a name to spark unconscious expectations is not to be underestimated.

The first names we will examine in this section are the ones we call the Power Names—those that conjure up someone smart or creative or energetic. The names in each of these three Power groups are distinct in tone and style, and your preference for one or the other will probably be clear, depending on your own hopes for your child's persona and talents.

Names can also project a physical image, not just of a person's attractiveness, but of the particular brand of appeal: sexy or pretty, refined or roguish. The force of names on people's perceptions of another's looks is well documented by studies outlined here, together with lists of names that have an attractive image.

Class is also an issue, albeit a touchy one, when it comes to a name's image. At any given time, some names are moving up the social ladder, improving their class standing, while others are moving down. Here you'll find today's upwardly mobile names, those that in the future can give your child a classy image.

Another image consideration is your child's position vis à vis his peers, how much his name will set him apart from the crowd or make him one of the gang. It's not difficult to pick the names at either extreme, but it's harder to define those that will help your child fit in and stand out. That's the list we present here. If you want to give your child an unusual name, will it help or harm him? We'll look at what psychologists have discovered about that. You'll also find a guide to names with images that may seem either too much or too little for a child to live up to.

And if the whole idea of a name's image defining your child appalls you, we offer here a selection of No Image names: those that have been used so frequently by such diverse groups of people that they present no clearly defined image of their own.

As a 5' 10½" teenager, Susan [Weaver] changed her name to Sigourney (a character in *The Great Gatsby*) because she thought that it better fit her height.

—*People* magazine, 1986

If your baby is a redhead, or you're hoping it will be, you may want to consider these names that mean red:

REED/READ/ REID   ROY
ROONEY   RUFUS
RORY   RUSKIN
ROSS   RUSSELL
ROWAN/ROHAN

POWER NAMES

The power of a name is often quite specific. Many strongly suggest a person who is particularly smart or energetic or creative. We have singled these out and call them the Power Names. Whether it is Intellectual Power, Creative Power, or High Energy, each has a potent image that can work for—or against—your child throughout his or her lifetime.

Some of this power comes from stereotypes: Martha the serious student and Bonnie the bouncy cheerleader. Sound also plays a part in imbuing names with power: Short, clipped names tend to suggest efficiency, for instance, while exotic or foreign names can have a creative, even a sexy ring.

Often, however, a name's power is drawn from more mysterious sources. But whatever its root, the image is unmistakeable. If you're in doubt, consider this: Of Helen, Kirstie, and Ariadne, who is the professor, who the gymnast, who the poet? While a Helen may very well do handsprings, a Kirstie lecture at Harvard, and an Ariadne negotiate loans, each will always be battling the image of her name.

Power names can be self-fulfilling prophecies. This is not because of some cabalistic force inherent in the name, but because it was chosen by parents who identify with the image the name projects. A painter and an actress, for instance, may prefer a name like Ariadne, with its creative undertones, over the kinetic Kirstie or the intellectual Helen for their child. Ariadne grows up in a house filled with her father's paintings, sees her mother perform on the stage, associates with the children of her parents' creative friends; is nurtured, in short, in a creative atmosphere. With that kind of background, she is likely to have a creative bent, no matter what her name.

Of course, naming your child Ariadne will not automatically make her creative. Power names say more about parents' expectations than they do about a child's talents. A child who has a different kind of power than her name suggests—the Ariadne who wants to grow up to be a businesswoman, or a gymnast—may feel, each time she says her name, that she is not what her parents hoped she would be. On the other hand, a power name can add dimension to one's personality with no effort on the part of its bearer. The numbers-crunching Ariadne, for instance, may enjoy being imagined "artistic" without ever having to set foot in a museum.

For their potential bonuses as well as burdens, you would do well to consider the following lists when choosing a name for your child.

INTELLECTUAL POWER NAMES

Names with Intellectual Power suggest someone who is not only intelligent but serious and studious. These are the kids who are always at the head of the class, who grow up to teach advanced logical positivism or study the gases of the outer atmosphere because it's fun.

We can't abandon you to this list without noting that we realize many of the names here seem, well, nerdy. It is unfortunate that an image of "smart" is often connected to an image of unattractive, boring, klutzy, or, in extreme cases, all three. The good news for these intellectual power names is that many are new arrivals on the fashion scene, which may actually be enough to make it cool to sound smart. Add twenty points to estimates of your child's IQ by naming her or him:

G I R L S

ADELE
ALICE
ANNA
BEATRICE
BERNICE
CAROLINE
CATHERINE/
   KATHERINE
CHARLOTTE
CLAIRE
CLAUDIA
CLORIS
CONSTANCE
CORA
DOROTHY
EDITH
ELEANOR
ESTHER
EVE
FAITH
FLORENCE
FRANCES

GILLIAN
GRACE
HANNAH
HARRIET
HELEN
HONOR
HOPE
IRENE
JANET
JUDITH
JULIA
KAY
LAURA
LEAH
LENORE
LOUISE
MADEL(E)INE
MARGARET
MARIAN
MARTHA
MIRIAM
NATALIE

NORA
NORMA
PAULA
PHILIPPA
PRUDENCE
RACHEL
REBECCA
ROSALIND
RUTH
SYDNEY
SYLVIA
THEODORA
VIRGINIA
VIVIAN
WINIFRED

B O Y S

ADLAI
ALBERT
ARTHUR
AUGUSTUS
BYRON
CHARLES
CLIVE
CONRAD
CYRIL
DREW
EL(L)IOT(T)
FRANKLIN
GILBERT
GORDON
HAROLD
HENRY
HOWARD
HUGH
JUSTIN
LAWRENCE
LEONARD
LINCOLN
MARSHALL
MAXWELL
MORTON
NATHAN
NELSON
NORMAN
OWEN
PAUL
PHIL(L)IP
QUINCY
RUPERT
SAUL
SOLOMON
SPENCER
STUART/STEWART
THEODORE
TRUMAN
WALTER
WINSTON

Sorry, Dawn, But Doris Got the Job

Sexy is not powerful, at least when it comes to a name that will get your daughter a good job. So suggests a master's thesis written by Deborah Linville while at Rensselaer Polytechnic Institute, which compared the relationship between "sexy" names and corporate hiring. Linville's conclusion: "The present study indicates that there is a prejudice regarding women applicants based on the degree of sexiness of their first names."

Names considered too sexy for executives, according to Linville's study, are: Adrienne, Andrea, Cheryl, Christine, Dawn, Erica, Heather, Jennifer, and Kathy. Names destined for corporate success include Alma, Cornelia, Doris, Ethel, Mildred, and Zelda.

CREATIVE POWER NAMES

Creative Power names tend to display a certain amount of creativity on the part of their bestowers: They are often unusual, exotic, sometimes foreign-sounding, sometimes associated with an artistic figure. Pablo sounds more creative than Pedro simply because of Picasso. Names with Creative Power set your child apart from the herd; from the beginning, he or she is seen as someone special. Any one of those listed here would not look out of place on a theater marquee or a book jacket, in a dance program or a gallery guide. Encourage your child's creativity with a name like:

GIRLS

ABRA	CLEA
ADRIA(NA)	CLEMENTINE
ALEXA	CLIO/CLEO
ALLEGRA	COLETTE
ANAIS	COLUMBINE
ANDRA	DAISY
AN(N)ABEL(LA)	DALLAS
ANTHEA	DAPHNE
ARABELLA	DARIA
ARDITH	DARYL
ARIADNE	DEIRDRE
ARIEL	DELIA
ASTRA	DEVON
AUDRA	DIANTHA
AURORA/AURELIA	DINAH
BARRA	DOMINIQUE
BETHANY	DORIAN
BIANCA	DYLAN
BLYTHE	ELECTRA
BREE	ESMÉ
BRONWYN/	EVANGELINE
BRONWEN	FELICITY
BRYN	FEODORA
CAMILLE/	FLANNERY
CAMILLA	FLAVIA
CANDIDA	FLEUR
CASSANDRA	FRANCESCA
CHELSEA	GABRIELLE/
CHINA	GABRIELLA
CHLOE	GELSEY

GEMMA	LILY
GENEVA	LOLA
GEORGIA(NA)	LUCIANA
GERMAINE	LULU
GISELLE	MACKENZIE
GREER	MAIA
GWYN/GWYNETH	MALA
ILANA/ILIANA	MARA
INDIA	MARGAUX
ISABEL(LA)	MARIEL
ISADORA	MARIS(S)A
IVY	MARLO
JADE	MARYA
JAEL	MAUD(E)
JASMINE	MERCEDES
JESSAMINE	MICHAEL/
JUSTINE	MICHAELA
KAIA	MINTA
KAYLA/KAILA	MIRABEL
KEZIA(H)	MIRANDA
KYLE	NADIA
KYRA	NATASHA/
LARA	NASTASSIA
LEATRICE	NEDDA
LEILA	NESSA
LELIA	NICOLA
LEONIE	ODELIA
LEYA	ODETTE
LIANA	OLIVIA
LILIANA	OPHELIA
LILITH	ORIANA
LILO	OUIDA

PALOMA
PERRY
PETRA
PHILIPPA
PHOEBE
PILAR
PORTIA
QUINTANA/
   QUINTINA
RAFFAELA
REINE
RENATA
SABINE
SABRA
SACHA/SASHA
SAVANNAH
SCARLETT
SHANA
SHOSHANA
SILVER
SIMONE
SKYE

SOPHIA
SYDNEY
TALIA
TALLULAH
TAMAR(A)
TANYA
TATIANA
TESS(A)
TRILBY
TWYLA
TYNE
VALENTINA
VENICE/VENETIA
VIOLET
WALKER
WILLA
WYNN(E)
ZANDRA
ZANE
ZARA
ZELIA
ZOE

B O Y S

ADRIAN
ALEXIS
ALISTAIR
AMYAS
ANATOL

ANDRÉ/ANDREAS
ANTON
BASIL
BEAU
BENNO

BOAZ	JEREMIAS
BORIS	JETHRO
CALEB	JONAH
CHRISTO	JOSIAH
CLAY	JULIAN
CLEMENT	KAI
CLOVIS	KELSEY
CODY	KENYON
COLE	KILIAN
COSMO	LIAM
CRISPIN	LIONEL
DALLAS	LONDON
DARIUS	LORENZO
D(I)MITRI	LORNE
DORIAN	LUCIAN
DYLAN	MACKENZIE
EBEN	MARCO
ELIAS	MARCUS
ELISHA	MARIUS
ELLERY	MERCE(R)
EMMETT	MICAH
EPHRAIM	MILO
EZRA	MISCHA
GABRIEL	MOSES
GARSON	MOSS
GIDEON	NATHANIEL
GRAY/GREY	NICO
HART	NOAH
INIGO	OMAR
JAMESON	ORLANDO
JARED	ORSON
JASPER	PABLO

PHILO   SIMON
PHINEAS   SKY
QUENTIN   THADDEUS
RAFAEL   THEO
RAOUL   TOBIAS
ROBIN   TRISTAN
SEBASTIAN

Creative class

Bennington College has long had the reputation of being a hotbed of creative activity. The following partial list of names of students, both male and female, enrolled there during a recent school year certainly reflects the creative activity of their parents during the naming process.

CHIARA
AMER   CIARAN
AMINA   DANIELIA
ANDERS   DECLAN
ANGHELIKA   DESIRÉE
ARIANE   EMORY
ARIELE   FAIZA
ARJUN   FAYNE
ARNIS   FELICITY
AURA   FLANNERY
BARNABAS   GHAZI
BERIL   GIBBS
BRENNA   GIOIA
BRYN   HYLA

IOANNIS
ITALIA
JOVITA
KAIJA
KALEB
KHEYA
LARA
LARISSA
LELLA
LIMORE
LORELIE
LYNMORE
MACEY
MAIYA
MANAL
MARYA
MAYA
MERCEDES

MERILEE
MIRI
MOLLIA
PARRISH
PIPER
RAFE
RHODY
RIO
RUSHA
SAVO
SCHUYLER
SEKKA
SHONA
SIMEON
TAMAR
TAMARA
VEENA
ZARAAWAR

HIGH-ENERGY NAMES

Names with physical power—High-Energy Names—fairly cartwheel off the tongue, conjuring up a person in constant motion. A disproportionate number of these names end in a long e sound, consistent with adjectives like bouncy and perky. At their peak in the early sixties—during JFK's "vigor" administration—many High Energy names will still serve a child well. You should be aware, however, that there is energy and then there's energy: the competent grownup kind suggested by names like Jill and Brady, and the pep-squad teenager variety personified by such names as Cindy and Tammy and Jamie, which often prove not enough to live up to. The difference between the two groups is readily apparent, and if you want a supercharged image of either kind, consider the following:

G I R L S

AILEEN	JAMIE
ALI/ALLY/ALLIE	JAN
AMY	JILL
ANNIE	JO
BARBIE	JODY
BETSY	JOLIE
BONNIE	JOY
CAREY/CARRIE	JULIE
CARLY	KEELY
CASEY	KELLY
CHRISTIE	KELSEY
CINDY	KERRY
DEBBIE	KIM
DENA	KIRSTIE
DIXIE	LAURIE
DOLLY	LEXIE
EILEEN	LINDA
ERIN	LISA
GAIL	LUCY
GAY	MARCY
GINNY	MELODY
GOLDIE	MERRY
HEIDI	MIMI
HOLLY	MINDY

MITZI
PATSY
PATTY
PEGGY
PENNY
PEPPER
PIPER
PIPPA
POPPY
RANDI
RICKI
RORY
ROXY

SHARI
SHELL(E)Y
SHERRY
STACEY
TAFFY
TAI
TAMMY
TATUM
TERRY
TRIXIE
VICKI
WENDY

B O Y S

ARI
BAILEY
BARNABY
BO
BOONE
BRADY
BRODY
CAREY
CASEY
COREY
DERRY
DEVLIN
EGAN
FLINT

HARDY
HOGAN
IAN
JAKE
JAMIE
JEREMY
JESSE
JODY
KELLY
KERRY
KIP
KIRK
KIT
LEO

LUKE	REX
MAC	RILEY
MAX	RORY
MICKEY	RYAN
MITCH	TERRY
PATRICK	TOBY
QUINN	TROY
REGGIE	ZACK
RENO	ZANE
REO	ZEBEDY

Reggie. Reginald Martinez Jackson: if this man were called Marty Jackson, he would be exactly three-fifths as famous as he is today. Reggie Jackson, with that repeating J, sounds right. And this: Reg-GIE. Reg-GIE. Reg-GIE.

It's the best hook in baseball.

—"Names of the game," by Rory Rebecca Metcalf and Gael Montgomery, *Village Voice,* August 26, 1986

BLIND DATE NAMES

Obviously it's beyond the power of a name to bestow good looks on your child—that, for better or worse, pretty much depends on genes, luck, and self-esteem. But a name with an attractive aura, like a good telephone voice, can influence other people's expectations and perceptions of someone's looks. Studies back this up: in one bogus beauty competition (see page 106), women of comparable attractiveness were rated with and without name tags. Nameless, the voting was even; when names became a factor, those with plain names were trounced by those with attractive ones.

An attractive name reinforces an attractive image, while an unattractive one contradicts it, can even throw it into question. We know a plain but charming man named Hunter who is wildly successful at getting dates, and admits he wouldn't be so lucky if his name were Melvin. On the other side of the coin is a perfectly nice-looking man named Herb who has, in desperation, resorted to introducing himself by his last name only—which happens to work as an appealing first name as well—and somehow doesn't get around to mentioning his given name until the third or fourth date.

ATTRACTIVE NAMES

Chances are, your sole criterion for a name isn't that it further your daughter's romantic career, but for better or worse, her name can have a lot to do with whether people see her as pretty or plain, foxy or frumpy.

Girls' names with a decidedly attractive image fall into two clear-cut groups: sexy and more delicately pretty. While a glamorous image, for example, will certainly spark your daughter's appeal on the blind-date circuit, you may want to think twice about the ways it will affect the other aspects of her life. Will Desirée make it to the boardroom? Studies say probably not.

The pretty names, however, carry less ambivalence. Some may be a tad soft, a bit flowery, but as a group they're more solidly grounded in the competent adult world.

Names that will arouse a certain anticipation in the opposite sex include:

S E X Y

AMBER	CLEO
APRIL	CRYSTAL
BAMBI	DAWN
BRANDY	DELILAH
BRITTANY	DESIRÉE
CHER	DOMINIQUE
CHRISTIE	FARRAH

GEORGIA
INDIA
JADE
JASMINE
LANA
LAUREN
LILA
LIZ
LIZA
LOLA
LOLITA
MARGAUX
MONIQUE

RAQUEL
RITA
SABRINE
SALOMÉ
SCARLETT
SELENA
STORM
TAMARA
TARA
TAWNY
TEMPEST
VERONIQUE

P R E T T Y

AMANDA
ADRIENNE
ALEXANDRA
AL(L)ISON
ANDREA
ANGELICA
ARIEL
ASHLEY
BRETT
BROOKE
CHLOE
COURTNEY
DEVON
DIANA

EDEN
FRANCESCA
GABRIELLE
HALEY/HAYLEY
HEATHER
HIL(L)ARY
JACQUELINE
JENNIFER
JESSICA
KATE
KIMBERLY
LAUREL
LESLIE
LINDSAY/LINDSEY

MARIEL   PA(I)GE
MELANIE   PAMELA
MELISSA   SABRINA
MIRANDA   SAMANTHA
MORGAN   TIFFANY
NATASHA   VANESSA
OLIVIA   WHITNEY

Call Me Claudette

Whenever a new girl joined up, the first thing she needed was a working name. . . .

To me, certain names have always suggested specific images. A girl named Natalie should have long dark hair. Alexandra is tall and stately, and Ginger is a spunky redhead. I gave the name Melody to a girl named Carol whose voice was so mellifluous it made me think of music. When Wilma joined up, tall, sophisticated, and experienced, I knew immediately that she would be Claudette. . . .

These new names weren't only for the comfort and convenience of the girls, they were equally important to those of us who had to describe the escorts over the phone. When I or one of the assistants was describing a girl to a client, we would have to conjure up an image of her in just two or three phrases. Her name could be a big help in that process.

One day I had the bright idea of buying one of those *What to Name Your Baby* books as a way to generate more names. . . . I wrote down a hundred or so names that I especially liked and started asking the new girls to make their selections from that list. . . .

Occasionally I would have to veto one of their suggestions, because names like Monique, Noelle, Nicole, and
Tiffany made a girl sound like a hooker. . . .

—Sydney Biddle Barrows with William Novak,
Mayflower Madam, Arbor House, 1986

Working Girls

Following is a list of names used by the call girls in Sydney
Biddle Barrows's employ, as cited in her book, *Mayflower
Madam:*

ADRIENNE	BARBARA
ALANNA	BIANCA
ALEXANDRA	BLAINE
ALEXIS	BLAKE
ALLISON	BOBBI
AMANDA	BREA
AMY	BRENT
ANGELA	BRITTAIN
ANNE	BROOKE I
ANNETTE	BROOKE II
ANYA	CAMERON
ARDEN	CAMILLE
ARIANA	CAREY
ARLENE	CARLA
ASHLEY	CAROLE
AUDREY	CAROLYN
AVERY	CATHY

CECELIA	ERICA
CELIA	GABRIELLA
CHANTAL	GINA
CHARLOTTE	GINGER
CHERYL	HEATHER I
CHRIS	HEATHER II
CHRISTY	HELENA
CLAIRE	IRENE
CLARISSA	JADE
CLAUDETTE	JAIME
COLBY	JANE
CORINNE	JANINE
DALE	JEANETTE
DANA	JEANNIE
DANIELLE	JENNIFER I
DARLENE	JENNIFER II
DEBBIE	JENNY
DEBRA	JERRI
DEEDEE	JESSICA
DEIDRE	JOANNA
DENISE	JODY
DEVIN	JUDY
DIANE	JULIA
DIDI	JULIE
DOMINIQUE	KAREN
DONNA	KATHERINE
DORIAN	KATY
DORY	KELLY I
EILEEN	KELLY II
ELAINE	KERRY
ELISE	KRISTEN
ELIZABETH	KRISTINE
EMILY	LAURA

LAURIE	PATTY
LEE	PAULA
LEIGH	PENNY
LENA	POLLY
LINDSAY	RAVIANA
LISA	REBECCA
LONNIE	ROBERTA
LORRAINE	ROBIN
LOUISE	SALLY
LYNNE	SANDY
MAGGIE	SEVERINE
MARGOT	SHARI
MARGUERITA	SHARON
MARIKO	SHAWNA
MARISA	SHELBY
MEGAN	SHELLEY
MEI	SHERRY
MELANIE	SHEVAUN
MELISSA I	SONYA
MELISSA II	SOPHIA
MICHELLE	STACEY
MILA	SUNNY
MITZI	SUSAN
MIYA	SUSIE
MONICA	SYLVIA
MONTGOMERY	TARA
NANCY	TAYLOR
NATALIA	TESS
NATALIE	TERRY
NATASHA	TINA
NICOLE	TRACEY
NINA	TRICIA
PAMELA	TRISH

VALERIE   VICKI
VANESSA   VICTORIA
VERONICA   WREN

Pretty Name, Pretty Woman

If you were shown a picture of a beautiful woman and told her name was Bertha, would that actually affect your response to her looks? The answer is a resounding yes, according to research conducted by psychologist S. Gray Garwood at Tulane University.

Garwood staged a mock "beauty contest" on the Tulane campus, using six pictures of women who had previously been judged equally attractive. Three of the contestants were given "desirable" names—Kathy, Jennifer, and Christine—and three were given "undesirable" ones—Ethel, Harriet, and Gertrude. (The names' desirability had been determined by a student survey conducted by Garwood a year earlier.)

The results: Kathy, Jennifer, and Christine garnered 158 votes, compared to only 39 for the unfortunate Ethel, Harriet, and Gertrude. Not only did the men find the attractively named women more attractive; the women voters did, too! The contestants with the "pretty" names received 83 percent of the male and 77 percent of the female vote.

> If parents really thought how much a name can influence a child's entire life, maybe they'd come up with better ones. Think about it. Is there a sex symbol named Erma? There is not! Is there a cheerleader in the Western world who answers to the name Erma? Get real. Are there any love songs, "Once in love with Erma"? Get outta here.

—Erma Bombeck, Los Angeles *Times* Syndicate, July 1986

HANDSOME NAMES

Good-looking names for boys can be divided into two categories: nice guys and not-so-nice guys. The nice guys are sensitive and sweet and tend to offer a goodnight kiss at the door; the rogues don't call the next morning, although women usually wish they would.

To facilitate your son's romantic future, consider the following when choosing a name:

H A N D S O M E   N I C E   G U Y S

ADAM	CAMERON
ADRIAN	CASEY
ALEX	CASS
BARNABY	COLIN
BEN	ERIC
BRYANT	ETHAN
CALVIN	EVAN

FORREST	MALCOLM
FRAZER	MAX
GABRIEL	MILO
GIDEON	NATHANIEL
GRANT	OLIVER
GREGORY	REED
GRIFFIN	REX
IAN	SAM
JARED	SCOTT
JED	SEAN
JEREMY	SIMON
JORDAN	THEO
JOSH	TOBIAS
JULIAN	TREVOR
JUSTIN	TYLER
KENYON	WADE
LOGAN	

HANDSOME ROGUES

ADDISON	CODY
ASH	DALLAS
AUSTIN	DALTON
BAILEY	DARCY
BEAU	DAVIS
BRADY	DENVER
BROCK	DEVON
BRONSON	DYLAN
CHAD	FLINT
CLAY	GAVIN
CLINT	GRAY

HART	PIERCE
HUNTER	QUINN
JACKSON	REX
JASPER	SEBASTIAN
JESSE	SHANE
JUDD	WILEY
KEIL	WOLF
LOGAN	WYATT
LUKE	ZACK
MACK	ZANE

Overheard by Bob Smith on Macy's main floor, one female shopper to another:

First shopper: He sounds very nice. What's his name?

Second shopper: Bernie . . . [slightly apologetic] . . . but he really doesn't look like a Bernie.

First shopper: So what does he look like?

Second shopper, happily: A Manny.

—Ron Alexander, "Metropolitan Diary," *The New York Times,* June 25, 1986

The name seems wrong for The Sexiest Man Alive—Harry is a name for an uncle, or a guy who asks you to the prom because his mother made him. Of course, Harold would be worse. So Harry it is. Harry Robinson Hamlin, to be precise—the Harry everyone's just wild about.

People magazine, March 30, 1987

Fitting in/
Standing out

Picture a nursery school classroom. In the middle of the room is a crowd of ordinary children—those with readily acceptable, blending-in names: the Jennifers and Jasons, the Johns and Janes. Pleasant and convivial, but a little, well, boring. Around the perimeter, standing or playing alone, are the children with names that are unusual, invented, eccentric—the Ravens and Rains, Ivos and Ianthes. Interesting but risky.

Running between the two groups—now blending in with the crowd, now standing out as individuals—are the children with names that are recognizable, yet not epidemic; unusual, but not weird.

Choosing a name that strikes this balance, that will help your child both fit in and stand out, is difficult. Names that do so successfully seem to fall into one of the following groups:

- Less common forms of classic names—Eliza instead of Elizabeth, for instance, or Ned rather than Edward.
- Classic names not widely used today—Philip and Grace, for example.
- Twists on trendy names—Laurel as opposed to Lauren, Alec for Alex.
- Fashionable names at the bottom of the most-popular lists, like Chelsea or Jeremy.

Names we consider to have found this golden mean include:

G I R L S

ABIGAIL	EMMA
ADRIENNE	EVE
AMELIA	GABRIELLA
BRIDGET	GEORGIA
CAMILLE	GILLIAN
CELIA	GRACE
CHELSEA	HANNAH
CHLOE	HIL(L)ARY
CHRISTA	JENNA
CLAIRE	JESSA
CLAUDIA	JOCELYN
COLETTE	JULIANA
DEIRDRE	JULIET
DINAH	KELSEY
DORIA	LACEY
ELENA	LARISSA
ELIZA	LAUREL

LEAH/LIA	PA(I)GE
LEILA	PAULINE
LILA	PHOEBE
LILY	POLLY
MADEL(E)INE	ROSANNA
MARA	ROSE
MARGO	SELENA
MARIETTA	SERENA
MARIS(S)A	SHEENA
MAURA	SIMONE
MEREDITH	SOPHIA
MIA	SOPHIE
MIRANDA	SUSANNAH
NATALIE	TAMAR(A)
NELL	TESS
NICOLA	TESSA
NINA	TOBY
NOELLE	VALENTINA
NORA	ZARA
OLIVIA	ZOE

B O Y S

ALEC	CODY
AUSTIN	DALLAS
BARNABY	DEREK
BRYANT	DREW
CALVIN	DUNCAN
CAMERON	EVAN
CLAY	GABRIEL

GREGORY	NOAH
GRIFFIN	OLIVER
HARRY	OWEN
HENRY	PATRICK
HUNTER	PHIL(L)IP
IAN	REED
JARED	ROSS
JED	SEBASTIAN
JEREMY	SETH
JONAH	SHANE
JUDD	SIMON
JULIAN	SPENCER
KYLE	TRAVIS
LEO	TREVOR
LUCAS	TROY
MALCOLM	TYLER
NATHANIEL	WADE
NED	ZANE

The best-liked names are those that are neither too common nor too unusual. So say a group of researchers at the University of Leicester in England, who have set forth the "Inverted U" (we would call it a bell curve) hypothesis. When names are either very familiar or very unfamiliar, according to the research, they are not very well liked, but at some intermediate level of familiarity, they achieve their peak popularity.

ODD NAME OUT?

To you, the name Waldo has worlds more character than William; Mabel is far more appealing than Michelle; Jessamine triumphs over Jessica hands down. But you worry about actually choosing one of these unusual, distinctive, even—yes—eccentric names for your child. Will little Waldo grow up to be a weirdo? Will Mabel be a nursery-school outcast?

No matter how much a champion of the individual you are, indelibly singling out your child with an odd name is a scary thing to do. You don't have to rely completely on guesswork to address your fears: There is a mass of research on how unusual names affect children. Some of the results are comforting. The bad news, however, is really awful:

When a boy named Carroll goes bad, he goes really bad.

Not to say Carls or Christophers don't commit crimes, too; it's just that, all things being equal, Carrolls commit more.

So suggest Drs. Robert C. Nicolay, A. Arthur Harman, and Jesse Hurley, psychologists at Loyola University in Chicago, who, over a five-year period, compared court psychiatric clinic cases of eighty-eight white males with unique names (really unique names like Oder, Lethal, and Vere) with eighty-eight others who had common names. Both groups had similar backgrounds and had committed similar crimes, but those with unusual names had perpetrated four times as many.

"Unique names interfere with normal social interaction and . . . this produces disturbed adjustment," the psychologists conclude. "When a child is given a name that causes embarrassment or confusion as to sex (such as Carroll), is the object of ridicule (Olive), or connotes snobbery (Brentwood), he is going to have to fight for it and this may create emotional problems."

However, we must point out that parents who named their child Lethal probably did not train him for a future in the helping professions.

Berthas and Elmers may get lower grades than Lisas and Michaels, not because they're less intelligent, but because teachers are prejudiced against their names.

Psychologists Herbert Harari and John McDavid asked eighty elementary-school teachers in San Diego to evaluate essays of similar quality on a relatively neutral subject ("What I Did Last Sunday"). The researchers arbitrarily assigned and switched around first names of the fifth- and sixth-grade authors. Sure enough, papers said to be written by children with names like Michael and David received a full grade higher than those of Elmer and Hubert, while Karen and Lisa got a grade and a half higher than Bertha.

Eccentric names breed eccentric kids.

It's a chicken-and-egg question, according to more than one study: Nonconformist parents give their child an unusual name and raise him in an out of the ordinary way. The kid then tries to live up to his name—and his parents' expectations—by becoming distinctive or eccentric.

Before you cross every unusual name off your list of possibilities, consider the opposing evidence:

In real life, the academic performance of Berthas and Elmers, Lisas and Michaels, has more to do with their brains than their names.

Contradicting the "essay study" cited above, psychologists compared the first names of 24,000 students in a midwestern city with their scores on a battery of Science Research Associates (SRA) tests.

The heartening conclusion: "[The data] clearly failed to support the hypothesis that unusual or unattractive names are generally or systematically associated with deficits in academic or social functioning."

Mabels fare better than Waldos, but both may have as good a shot as any kid of doing just fine, thank you.

Girls are more apt than boys to find social acceptance and so avoid psychological problems because of having unusual names, according to research done at the Northern New Jersey Mental Hygiene Clinic by psychologists Albert Ellis and Robert M. Beechley.

Also, girls are more likely than boys to have unusual names, are more likely to find that other people like their names, and are more likely to score high marks on self-acceptance tests, according to Richard L. Zweigenhaft of Guilford College.

After carrying out a study in which he found that of those people listed in both the Social Register and *Who's Who in America,* 70 percent had unusual names and only 23 percent had common names, Zweigenhaft concluded: ". . . in certain settings (such as the upper class provides) and with certain criteria (such as achievement), having an unusual first name does not have a detrimental effect and might even have a beneficial one."

If you want to give your child of either sex an unusual name, we suggest you focus on another of Zweigenhaft's conclusions: "Neither men nor women appear to be at a psychological disadvantage as a result of having an unusual or sexually ambiguous first name."

The Real Reason Movie Stars Don't Live in France

French parents who give their children unusual names like Jade or Cerise are not just taking chances with their children's psyches; they're breaking the law.

An 1803 law drafted under Napoleon, who disliked eccentric names (wonder why?), gives the government final say over parents' choices of names. And if a name is "ridiculous" or "likely to provoke teasing," the court has the power to throw it out and substitute one it deems more suitable.

Judged illegal in recent years have been Prune, Jade, Cerise, Manhattan, and Fleur de Marie. Also rejected recently was, ironically enough, Napoleon—not because of the name itself, but because the child's last name was Lempereur (the emperor). Explained the mayor who turned it down: "We thought it would be just too hard for the little kid to take."

—*The Wall Street Journal,* June 10, 1987

Names are really important. In fact there's something I've never been able to figure out. When a child gets an unusual name, does he or she unconsciously try to live up to it? Or is a name a destiny over which he or she has no control?

Did little Fawn shred paper dolls instead of cutting them up with scissors? Did Tammy like to play dress-up and get into mama's makeup when she was 3? Did Imelda exchange credit cards as a little girl like some boys exchanged base-ball cards?

It's my theory that the unusual name was deliberate because mothers thought it would take their offspring out of the ordinary and set them on a path bound for fame.

—Erma Bombeck, Los Angeles *Times* Syndicate,
July 1986

CLASS STANDING

You want to give your child a name with class, a name that will imbue him or her with an aura of good breeding and refined taste. Even if you're not striving to create an impression of great wealth, at least you don't want to saddle your kid with a name that conjures up trailer parks and greasy spoons.

But class is a sticky issue, and a name's status on the social ladder is constantly shifting. Trying to cipher the current class standing of a name can be as difficult as figuring out how much money Donald Trump really has. A few general rules of thumb, however, will provide basic guidance.

- Most names of obscenely rich television characters (Alexis, Blake, Krystle) are downwardly mobile, as are names of obscenely rich real people (for example, Morgan and Whitney) unless you really are a Morgan or a Whitney.
- Also downwardly mobile are names of ridiculously expensive stores or things: Tiffany, Bentley, or Crystal, for instance.

- On the other hand, names used for servants in 1930s movies about obscenely rich people are now upwardly mobile. Bridget, Josephine, Rose, Tillie, Amos, and Patrick have all arrived at the front door.
- Also climbing America's social ladder are eccentric names long favored by British nobility, names like Dinah, Jemima, Sophie, Harry, and Ralph.
- Names more obviously redolent of British nobility, like Amanda, Courtney, and Ashley, are downwardly mobile, however, as are names dripping with Frenchness—Michelle, Danielle, Nicole.
- Upwardly mobile are more homespun ethnic names—Irish, Italian, and Jewish favorites like Margaret, Maria, and Max.
- Also on the way up are plain, quiet names—Jane and John, Nora and Jack—that reflect the current status of conservative living and traditional taste.

These topsy-turvy rules are confusing, yes, but they are based on social principles that can be applied to other things—clothes, furniture, cities—as well as names. Here's how it works: The elite choose names sanctioned by their own social milieu, the middle class imitates the elite, and the working class imitates the middle class. But once a name filters down to the hoi polloi and becomes common, in both senses of the word, the classy image that sparked its popularity is tarnished and it falls out of favor first with the upper class, then with the middle, then with the lower. (Numerous examples of names that quite recently suggested an aura of class, of money and privilege, but are now downwardly mobile will be found in the section on names that are So Far In They're Out.)

The Upwardly Mobile names that are listed below are for the most part ones that have long been relegated to the lower rungs but whose image is rising, and rapidly. Previously in the mansion's kitchen or out in the fields, these Upwardly Mobile names are now more and more likely to be heard in the nursery.

Upwardly mobile names

G I R L S

AGNES	HANNAH
ALICE	HARRIET
ANNA	HELEN
AN(N)ABEL(LE)	HENRIETTA
BEATRICE	ISABEL(LA)
BERNADETTE	IVY
BESS	JANE
BRIDGET	JASMINE
CHARLOTTE	JEMIMA
CHRISTABEL	JOSEPHINE
CLAIRE	LILY
CLEMENTINE	LOLA
CLEO	LOUISE
CLOVER	MADEL(E)INE
DAISY	MAE/MAY
DELILAH	MAGGIE
DINAH	MAMIE
EDITH	MARGARET
ELEANOR	MARIA
FLORA	NATALIE
FRANCES	NELLIE
GEORGIA	NORA

OLIVE
PATRICIA
PHOEBE
POLLY
ROSE
SADIE
SALLY

SONIA
SOPHIE
STELLA
TESS
TILLIE
VIOLET

B O Y S

AMOS
BEN(JAMIN)
CALEB
CALVIN
EDWARD
FELIX
FRANCIS
FREDERICK
GEORGE
GUS
HARRY
HENRY
JACK
JAMES

JASPER
JOHN
LEO
MACK
MAX
NATHAN
PATRICK
RALPH
SAM(UEL)
SILAS
SIMON
TRAVIS
WILL

NAMES THAT ARE TOO MUCH, OR NOT ENOUGH, TO LIVE UP TO

Some names are so godlike, so heroic, that they could easily crush a tiny ego before it has a chance to sprout. On the other side of the coin are the names that even a toddler can transcend, names better suited to a parakeet than a person. Beware of giving your child a name that is either too much to live up to, or one he or she will always have to struggle to rise above.

Too much to live up to

ACHILLES   ARISTOTLE
AJAX   ATLAS
AMADEUS   BLISS
ANTIGONE   CAESAR
APHRODITE   CASSANDRA

CHASTITY	OBEDIENCE
CLEOPATRA	OCTAVIUS
CONAN	ODYSSEUS
DANTE	OPHELIA
DESIRÉE	ORESTES
FIDEL	PLATO
GLORY	RADCLIFFE
GOLIATH	RAMBO
HAMLET	REMBRANDT
HERCULES	RHETT
JESUS	ROMEO
JEZEBEL	SALOME
LAFAYETTE	STARR
LANCELOT	STORM
LAZARUS	TEMPERANCE
LOTHARIO	TEMPEST
LUCRETIA	VENUS
MAXIMILIAN	WASHINGTON
MERLIN	WELLINGTON
MUHAMMED	ZOLTAN
NAPOLEON	

Not enough to live up to

BABE	BIRDY
BABETTE	BITSY
BAMBI	BRANDI/BRANDY
BARBI(E)	BUBBLES
BIFF	BUCK

BUD	MINDY
BUNNY	MISSIE
CANDY	MUFFIN
CHERRY	MUFFY
CHIP	PEPPER
CINDY	PIP
DEE	POPPY
DODY	RICKY
DOLLY	RIP
DOM	SHEP
DUKE	SHERRY
DUSTY	SISSY
FAWN	SKIP
FLIP	SONNY
GOLDIE	SUNNY
GYPSY	TAB
HY	TAD
IKE	TAFFY
JUNIOR	TAMMY
KIT	TAWNY
LES	TIPPI
LUCKY	TISH
MIDGE	ZERO
MIMI	

I always thought of myself as a star . . . I knew I was born to it . . . I think people are named names for certain reasons, and I feel that I was given a special name for a reason. In a way, maybe I wanted to live up to my name.

—Madonna, quoted by Stephen Holder, *The New York Times,* June 29, 1986

No-image Names

What do you think of when you hear the name James? It could be someone as sullenly sexy as James Dean or as smoothly sophisticated as James Bond. In other words, a James, like a John, Jack, or Joseph, can be anything. And, indeed, some names are chosen precisely because they project no specific personality. We asked two mothers we know why they had named their sons Michael, currently the most common boys' name in America. Both gave almost the same reply: With a name shared by so many different types of men comes a certain freedom for the child to be whatever he wants to be. Enough genetic destiny would be imposed on their sons, they felt, without the further constriction of a type-casting name.

But popularity is not enough to guarantee anonymity. Some of today's most-used names—in particular romantically feminine girls' names such as Jessica, Heather, and Amanda—evoke specific expectations.

Names that are truly "no image" tend to be those used over long periods of time by parents from a cross section of religious, class, and ethnic backgrounds. Most are either short and unadorned or have so many nickname possibilities that there would be one to fit any kind of child.

G I R L S

ANN(E)	JOAN
BARBARA	KATE
CAROL	LEIGH/LEE
ELIZABETH	LYNN
ELLEN	NANCY
JANE	PATRICIA
JEAN	SALLY
JENNY	SUSAN

B O Y S

ALAN	MARK
ANDREW	MATTHEW
CHARLES	MICHAEL
CHRISTOPHER	NICHOLAS
DANIEL	PAUL
DAVID	PETER
EDWARD	RICHARD
JACK	ROBERT
JAMES	STEPHEN
JOHN	THOMAS
JOSEPH	WILLIAM

Mikes, Petes, Sams, Johns, Als, and Bills can grow up to be almost anything they want, while Keiths and Summers have to battle heavy odds to avoid careers in dental caps.

—Russell Baker, "A Name for All Seasons," Sunday Observer, *The New York Times,* October 21, 1984

[To my father] there were still numbers of names which hung so equally in the balance before him that they were absolutely indifferent to him. Jack, Dick and Tom were of this class: These my father called neutral names;—affirming of them . . . that there had been as many knaves and fools at least, as wise and good men, since the world began, who had indifferently borne them. . . . Bob, which was my brother's name, was another of these neutral kinds of Christian names, which operated very little either way; . . . Andrew was something like a negative quality in Algebra with him—'twas worse, he said, than nothing—William stood pretty high—and Nick, he said, was the Devil.

—Laurence Sterne, *Tristram Shandy,* 1759

SEX

This section will solve all your sexual problems—at least in the area of naming your child.

Here is where we consider the gender implications of names—from the ultrafeminine to the tomboyish, from the macho to the wimpy—as well as the ever-increasing territory of ambisexual names in between.

When considering names for your baby, you may not have identified sex as the factor that makes one group of names sound appealing to you, another repellent. But most names do have a clear sexual identity, do suggest different degrees of masculinity or femininity. And the fact is that the name you select casts a distinct reflection of how strongly feminine or masculine you want your child to be and appear. If you are suggesting boys' names like Spencer and Miles, and your husband is countering with Rod and Clint, sooner or later he will accuse you of trying to turn your son into a wimp and you will tell him that's better than producing a baby who wears boxing gloves.

We are aware that the sexual reading of names can be subjective. Reactions will be generational (someone picturing the young Dorothy Lamour might wonder how that name ever got into the no-frills category) and individual (you dated a fullback named Dwight in high school and have forever after considered it the most masculine name in the world). You'll be surprised, however, by how many names—because of sound, style or specific connotation—have very distinct sexual profiles.

Your feelings about the sexual image of girls' names may be influenced by your stand on feminist issues. One father we interviewed said that in looking for a name for their daughter, he and his wife applied the following test: Does this sound like a prospective justice of the Supreme Court? As more and more women enter the work force, many parents are seeking an androgynous or no-frills name that will give their daughter an edge with the male competition.

As ambisexual names increase in popularity for girls, however, more parents are looking for traditionally masculine names for boys. While a name like Ashley sounds strong and capable for a girl, it has now lost a certain degree of power as a boy's name. Even the new manly names that reflected the sensitized ideal male image of the seventies are—and we think this may be a sad step backward—declining under the pressures of our brave new world.

One way to approach this section is to consider these issues first and find names that appeal to you and reflect your position. Another option is to draw up a list of names that you like and then use our classifications to make sure their gender implications are the ones you had in mind.

Either method will help you discover the kind of sexual identity you would like your child to project to the world: the daintiness of a Cicely, the sultriness of a Selena, or the briskness of a Bess; the brute force of a Flint or the sensitivity of a Seth.

I find it entirely appropriate that Sofka should have named her sons after kings and emperors and her daughters as if they were characters in a musical comedy. Thus were their roles designated for them. The boys were to conquer, the girls to flirt. . . . Sofka sees her children's futures as being implicit in their names.*

—Anita Brookner, *Family and Friends,*
Pantheon Books, 1985

*Those names were Frederick, Alfred, Mireille (Mimi), and Babette (Betty).

FROM MADONNA
TO MERYL

The sexual impact of girls' names seems to break down into four main categories:

Feminissima: The ultrafeminine, often sexy, sometimes fluffy female names, à la Madonna.

Feminine: Female names that suggest a classic sort of femininity.

No-frills: Straightforward names that, while clearly female, have an efficient, no-nonsense air.

Boyish: Names like Meryl that are used for girls but have a boyish or ambisexual image.

Here you'll find specifics on each of these categories, along with lists of names in the four groups. In addition, if there is a girl's name you like, but you're not comfortable with its sexual image, we offer a guide to modifying the name to make it fit into a more acceptable category.

Now I wonder what would please her,
Charlotte, Julia or Louisa?
Ann and Mary, they're too common;
Joan's too formal for a woman:
Jane's a prettier name beside;
But we had a Jane that died.
They would say, if 'twas Rebecca,
That she was a little Quaker,
Edith's pretty, but that looks
Better in old English books.
Ellen's left off long ago:
Blanche is out of fashion now.
None that I have named as yet
Are so good as Margaret.
Emily is neat and fine.
What do you think of Caroline?
—Charles Lamb, 1809

FEMINISSIMA NAMES

If these names were dresses, they would be pale pink, with ruffles and lace and big bows and sprigs of flowers strewn on every available square inch. They are the sweetest of the sweet, the most feminine of the feminine names.

What makes these names Feminissima rather than merely Feminine? Three or more syllables sometimes do it. Soft sounds—s's and f's—can also push a name over the edge from Feminine to Feminissima. Names that by their meaning suggest ultrafeminine qualities, like Allegra and Lacey, are Feminissima. Very exotic names—especially Latin ones like Raffaela and Gabriella—qualify. And sex-goddess names—from Salomé to Marilyn to Madonna—also connote an exaggerated femininity.

You can hardly give your daughter one of these names without suggesting a little girl with ringlets and rosy cheeks, the kind of child who plays only with dolls (with ringlets and rosy cheeks) and cries if her Mary Janes get scuffed. Her name will make boys want to go on blind dates with her, and other girls see her as a potential threat even before they meet her.

Does that mean that giving your girl a Feminissima name will automatically make her a spineless jellyfish? Quite the opposite. There is something modern about these hyperfeminine names, something liberating about the possibility of an Angelica being chosen vice-president over an Alix. Just as the notion of a female Tyler with long hair and high heels has the appeal of the unexpected, so has that of a Felicia in a business suit or sweat pants.

Feminissima names

ADORA	ANGELINA
ADRIANA	ANNABELLA
ALEXANDRA	ARABELLA
ALLEGRA	ARIANA
ALYSSA and	ARIEL
variations	AURORA
ANGELICA	BABETTE

BARBIE	JOSETTE
BELINDA	JULIANA
BLOSSOM	LACEY
CAMILLA	LANA
CAROLINA	LARISSA
CASSANDRA	LETITIA
CECILIA	LILIANA
CECILY	LISABETH
CHERIE	LOUELLA
CHRISSIE	LUCIANA
CHRISTABEL	LUCINDA
CICELY	MADONNA
CLARISSA	MARCELLA
CRYSTAL	MARIETTA
DAWN	MARILYN
DESIRÉE	MELISSA
DOLLY	MELODY
ELISSA	MERRY
EMMALINE	MIRABELLE
EVANGELINE	MISSIE
FAWN	MONIQUE
FELICIA	ORIANA
FIFI	PANDORA
FRANCESCA	PANSY
GABRIELLA	PRISCILLA
GEORGIANA	RAFFAELA
GISELLE	ROSALINDA
HEATHER	SABINA
HYACINTH	SABRINA
ISABELLA	SALOMÉ
JESSICA	SAMANTHA

SCARLETT	TEMPEST
SELENA	TIFFANY
SERENA	TRICIA
SUZETTE	VALENTINA
TABITHA	VANESSA
TAFFY	VENUS
TATIANA	YVETTE

Baby Boom stars [Diane] Keaton as J.C. "We figured the character had a name she never liked—too feminine," explains Meyers. "You know, like Nanci—with the *i.*"

—Producer Nancy Meyers, quoted in *Elle,* October 1987

FEMININE NAMES

By far the largest group of girls' names is made up of Feminine names: names that are clearly female without being too fussy, sweet without being syrupy, soft without being limp. Many of the most popular girls' names of recent years can be found on this list. Style has favored these decidedly feminine names, along with androgynous names, over either ultrafeminine or no-nonsense female names.

The advantages of a Feminine name are several. Most of these names are easy to understand and easy to like: Your child will hear again and again what a pretty name she has, and that's pleasing. Also, kids like names that are sexually unambiguous; they like labels that clearly identify them as a girl or a boy. And most of these names are familiar, either because of their classic status or because they have been popular in recent times.

What of the future for Feminine names? Some, like Katherine and Elizabeth, are virtually timeless, but many of the names in this group have been so fashionable for several years that they verge on the cliché. If you want to stay away from a name that is already too trendy, be sure to cross-reference any you like here with the So Far In They're Out list in the Style section. One general observation: Many of the hypereuphonic feminine names—Jennifer, Christina, et al—are on their way out, while more offbeat feminine names, like Annabel, Daisy, Savannah, sound newer and stronger.

Feminine names

ABIGAIL	AMBER
ADELA	AMELIA
ADELAIDE	AMY
ADELINE	ANDREA
ADRIENNE	ANGELA
AILEEN	AN(N)ABEL(LE)
ALANA/ALANNA	ANNETTE
ALEXA	ANTONIA
ALEXANDRA	APRIL
ALEXIS	ARAMINTA
ALICIA	AUDRA
AL(L)ISON	AUDREY
AMANDA	BEATRICE

BEATRIX
BECCA
BELLE
BERNADETTE
BIANCA
BONNIE
BRIDGET
BRONWYN/
   BRONWEN
CAITLIN
CAMILLE
CANDACE
CARA
CAROLINE
CATHERINE/
   KATHERINE
CELESTE
CELIA
CHELSEA
CHLOE
CHRISTA
CHRISTIANA
CHRISTINA
CHRISTINE
CLARICE
CLAUDETTE
CLEMENTINE
COLETTE
COLLEEN
CORDELIA
CORNELIA

CYNTHIA
DAISY
DANIELLA
DAPHNE
DARLA
DARLENE
DEANNA
DEBORAH
DEIRDRE
DELIA
DELILAH
DENISE
DIANA
DINAH
DOMINIQUE
DONNA
DORA
DOREEN
DORIA
DOROTHEA
EILEEN
ELAINE
ELENA
ELISE
ELIZA
ELIZABETH
ELOISE
EMILY
ESMÉ
EVA
EVELYN

FERN
FIONA
FLORA
FRANCINE
GABRIELLE
GAY
GELSEY
GEORGIA
GILLIAN
GINA
GLORIA
GLYNIS
GRETCHEN
GWENDOLYN
HALEY/HAYLEY
HELENA
HELENE
HENRIETTA
HIL(L)ARY
HOLLY
IMOGEN(E)
INGRID
IRIS
ISABEL
JACQUELINE
JANICE
JANINE
JASMINE
JEANETTE
JENNA
JENNIFER

JESSA
JOANNA
JOCELYN
JULIA
JULIET
JUSTINE
KATHLEEN
KEZIA(H)
KIMBERLY
KIRSTEN
KRISTIN
LANA
LARA
LAURA
LAUREL
LAUREN
LEATRICE
LEILA
LEONORA
LIA
LIANA
LILA
LILIAN
LILY
LINDA
LISA
LIZA
LOLA
LORETTA
LORNA
LORRAINE

LOUISA	NOELLE
LUCIA	NOREEN
LUCY	ODELIA
MADEL(E)INE	ODESSA
MARA	ODETTE
MARCIA/MARSHA	ODILE
MARGO	OLIVIA
MARGUERITE	OPHELIA
MARIA	PALMA
MARIEL	PALOMA
MARINA	PAMELA
MARLENE	PATRICIA
MARYA	PAULETTE
MAURA	PAULINA
MAUREEN	PAULINE
MEGAN	PEGEEN
MELANIE	PENELOPE
MERCEDES	PETRA
MIA	PHILIPPA
MICHELLE	PHOEBE
MIRANDA	PIA
MOLLY	PILAR
MONICA	POLLY
NANCY	QUINTINA/
NANETTE	QUINTANA
NAOMI	RAMONA
NATALIE	REBECCA
NESSA	REGINA
NICOLA	RENATA
NICOLE	RENÉE
NINA	RHEA

RITA
ROCHELLE
ROSA
ROSALIE
ROSALIND
ROSAMOND
ROSANNA
ROSEMARY
ROWENA
ROXANNE
RUBY
SABINE
SABRA
SANDRA
SAVANNAH
SELENA
SERENA
SHANA
SHANNON
SHARON
SHEENA
SHEILA
SHERRY
SHIRA
SHOSHANA
SIMONE
SONDRA
SONIA
SOPHIA
STELLA
STEPHANIE
SUSANNAH

SUZANNE
SYLVIA
TALIA
TAMAR
TAMARA
TANYA
TARA
TESSA
THEODORA
T(H)ERESA
TILLIE
TINA
TRISH
VALERIE
VENICE/VENETIA
VERONICA
VICTORIA
VIOLET
VIRGINIA
VIVIAN
WENDY
YASMINE
YOLANDA
YVONNE
ZANDRA
ZARA
ZELIA
ZENA
ZIA
ZOE
ZORAH

NO-FRILLS NAMES

These are the denim skirts of girls' names: clearly not fit for boys, but as straightforward, down to earth, and—sometimes—blunt as you can get while still being female.

One readily apparent difference between these and the more feminine girls' names is that they are shorter: fewer letters and syllables, fewer embellishments. Many end in consonants rather than vowels, which gives them a harder sound. They're almost like generic labeling: Yes, they say, this is a girl, but that's all we're going to tell you.

The No-Frills names here fall into two groups: those with a straightforward sound—direct and to-the-point names like Jean, Lynn, Ruth—and those with a no-nonsense image: Constance, Gladys, Mildred.

While names from both groups have been out of favor for several years now, many are on their way back into style. Trend-setters are already adopting some of them: Sam Shepard and Jessica Lange's baby daughter is named Hannah Jane; Meryl Streep's daughters are named Grace Jane and Mary Willa, and Willa is also the name of Lindsay Crouse and David Mamet's daughter. We've heard of some stylish young Eleanors and Helens and Josephines as well.

Some of these names, however, are still struggling against a residual image of dowdiness, and you'll see them on our So Far Out They'll Probably Always Be Out list, starting on page 35. Others—Ellen, Carol, Barbara, for instance—were popular quite recently, and won't be due for a comeback until ranch houses and avocado green refrigerators are back in style. But with fifties blond-wood furniture selling for high prices in Greenwich Village, that may be sooner than you'd guess.

No-frills names

ADA
ADELE
AGATHA
AGNES
ALICE
ANNA
ANN(E)
BARBARA
BERNICE
BERTHA
BESS
BETH
BLANCHE
CARLA
CAROL
CASS
CEIL
CHARLOTTE
CLAIRE
CLAUDIA
CONSTANCE
CORA
CORINNE
DELLA
DIANE
DORA
DORCAS
DORIS

DOROTHY
EDITH
EDNA
ELEANOR
ELLA
ELLEN
EMMA
ENID
ESTELLE
ESTHER
ETHEL
ETTA
EUNICE
EVE
FAITH
FAY
FRANCES
FRIEDA
GAIL
GERALDINE
GLADYS
GRACE
GRETA
GWEN
HANNAH
HARRIET
HAZEL
HEIDI

HELEN	LOUISE
HESTER	LUCILLE
HILDA	LYNN
HONOR	MADGE
HOPE	MAE/MAY
HORTENSE	MAEVE
IDA	MARGARET
INA	MARIAN
INEZ	MARIE
IRENE	MARTHA
JANE	MARY
JANET	MAUD(E)
JEAN	MAVIS
JILL	MAXINE
JOAN	MEG
JOANNE	MILDRED
JOSEPHINE	MIRIAM
JOY	MONA
JOYCE	NELL
JUDITH	NOLA
JULIE	NORA
JUNE	NORMA
KAREN	OLIVE
KATE	PATIENCE
KAY	PAULA
KIM	PAULINE
LEAH	PEARL
LEIGH	PHYLLIS
LENORE	PRUDENCE
LESLIE	RACHEL
LOIS	RHODA

ROBERTA
ROSE
RUTH
SADIE
SALLY
SARA(H)
SELMA
SOPHIE
SUSAN
SYBIL

THELMA
TRUDY
VELMA
VERA
VERNA
WANDA
WILLA
WINIFRED
ZELDA

BOYISH NAMES

Whitney Houston has one. So do Glenn Close, Meryl Streep, Jodie Foster, Brooke Shields, Daryl Hannah, Mel Harris, Mackenzie Phillips, Michael Learned, Lindsay Wagner, Bo Derek, Drew Barrymore, Quinn Cummings, Barrie Chase, Norris Church, and Christopher Norris. Jamie Lee Curtis has two.

They're Boyish names, and they're increasingly popular for girls. Time was, women hid behind men's names in order to be taken seriously. But where George—as in Eliot or Sand—was once an alias, now it's more likely to be a girl's real name.

There is a long history of appealing heroines with boyish names: from Jo in *Little Women* to Lady Brett in *The Sun Also Rises*. In fact, there are dozens of leading ladies who have played a character with a masculine-sounding name at some point in their careers. Irene Dunne was Ray, for example, and Audrey Hepburn, Reggie; Tuesday Weld, Christian; Bette Davis, Stanley; Olivia DeHavilland, Roy; Janet Leigh, Wally; and Jane Russell, Nancy Sinatra, and Anne Baxter all Mikes.

Television loves Boyish names for girls: you can watch Rudy on "The Cosby Show" or Mallory on "Family Ties" or Blair on "The Facts of Life" or Alexis on "Dynasty." The night and daytime soaps are rife with female Kirbys, Sydneys and Blaines. And several celebrities have chosen Boyish names for their daughters: Sissy Spacek's little girl is named Schuyler, for instance, and one of Bill Cosby's daughters is called Evin.

Sometimes, a name that sounds tired for a boy, like Sydney, becomes fresh and crisp when applied to a girl. Names that can be wimpy for a boy, such as Brooke or Blair, can confer a brisk kind of strength on a girl.

But Boyish names often appeal more to parents than to the child herself. A girl named Casey may be disturbed by the fact that her male playmate down the block has the same name, and wish she were called something more clearly defined as female, like Jennifer. However, most grown-up women with Boyish names say they began to be grateful to their parents for them when they reached the age of about eighteen. At that point, they started to appreciate the sexual ambiguity as well as the sex appeal of having a boyish name.

What follows is a list of Boyish names that are commonly used for girls. If you want to venture further into masculine-sounding names for your daughter, also consult the list of ambisexual names, starting on page 176.

Boyish names

ALI	ASHLEY
ALIX/ALEX	BARRIE
ALLY/ALLIE	BERRY

BERYL	JODY
BILLIE	JORDAN
BLAIR	KEIL
BO	KELLY
BRETT	KELSEY
BROOKE	KERRY
BRYN	KIM
CAREY	KIT
CARLIN	KYLE
CARLY	LEE
CARMEN	LESLIE
CASEY	LINDSAY
CHRIS	MACKENZIE
CODY	MALLORY
COREY	MEREDITH
COURTNEY	MERLE
DALE	MERYL
DANA	MORGAN
DEVON	NOEL
DORIAN	PAT
EDEN	RAE
FLANNERY	RANDI/RANDY
GENE	RICKI/RICKY
GERMAINE	ROBIN
GERRY	RORY
GREER	SACHA/SASHA
GWYN	SHAWN
JAMIE	SHELBY
JAN	SHELL(E)Y
JESSIE	SYDNEY
JO	TERRY

TOBY	WALLIS
TRACY	WHITNEY
TRILBY	WYNN
TYNE	

We don't know any boys named Sue, but we sure do know a lot of girls named Alex. That seems to be the screenwriters' female moniker of choice these days. We've seen Jennifer Beals as Alex Owens in *Flashdance*, Jane Fonda as Alex Sternbergen in *The Morning After*, Debra Winger as Alex Barnes in *Black Widow*, and Cher as Alex Medford in *The Witches of Eastwick*. Most recently, Glenn Close (who was named Teddy in her last movie, *Jagged Edge*) joined the ranks, playing Alex Forrest in *Fatal Attraction*.

—*Premiere* magazine, December 1987

FROM CLARISSA TO CARSON

You don't have to give up on a girl's name entirely because it's either too pink or too blue for your taste. Sometimes a slight twist can change a name from Feminissima to Feminine to No Frills to Boyish, or back again. Here are some names that, with a few changes, can span the degrees of femininity:

ADORA	ADRIANA
DORIA	ADRIENNE
DORIS	ADELE
DORIAN	ADDISON

ALEXANDR(I)A
ALEXA
ALEXIS
ALEX

CLARISSA
CLARICE
CARLA
CARSON

ALYSSA
ALISON
ALICE
ALI

ELISSA
ELIZA
ELLEN
ELLERY

BELINDA
LINDA
LYNN
LINDSAY

EMMALINE
EMILY
EMMA
EMLYN

CAROLINA
CAROLINE
CAROL
CAREY

FRANCESCA
FRANCINE
FRANCES
FRANKIE

CASSANDRA
CELESTE
CASS
CASEY

HYACINTH
VIOLET
ROSE
IVY

CECILY
CELIA
CEIL
CLEO

LOUELLA
LOUISA
LOUISE
LOU

MARIETTA
MARIEL
MARY
MERYL

MELISSA
MELANIE
NELL
MEL

TIFFANY
T(H)ERESA
TESS
TERRY

FROM RAMBO
TO SYLVESTER

Boys' names can be divided into four major gender categories. These are:

Macho: Names so hypermasculine they conjure up a frame from *Pumping Iron.*

Manly: The classic male names, used consistently over the centuries, suggesting traditional and clear-cut masculinity.

New manly: Boys' names that have burgeoned in popularity in the postfeminist era. While clearly masculine, these names nonetheless suggest a new, enlightened sort of man.

Wimpy: Sorry, Sylvester, but you're one of the group of male names with a weak image.

In this section, you'll find more details on what these categories mean, as well as lists of names that fall into each one. Also here is a list of macho men who triumphed over their wimpy names, as well as a section on male names whose sexual image is shifting.

MACHO NAMES

If *First Blood* was your favorite movie and you're hoping for a little boy who'll strut through the world toting a plastic machine gun and pulling a toy tank, then one of these supermacho names is for you. But remember that even if your little Rod or Bart doesn't look or act like a bull on testosterone, he will always be measured against his name. Girls will giggle, boys will flex their muscles, and nursery-school teachers will wring their hands in anticipation.

Of course, a good many of these names have become jokes: Not many people would name their infant son Attila or Zoltan. But even the more reasonable names carry a lot of hypermasculine baggage. Giving your baby boy one of these macho names is like handing him a football, a hockey stick, and a baseball bat in the nursery and expecting him to play extremely well, or else.

Little Rod or Bart may rebel, the way some particularly well-known guys named Bruce, Arnold, and Sylvester have, but with less desirable consequences. For more on the contrary effect names can have on sexuality, see "Don't Pick a Fight with Bruce," page 172.

Macho names

ANGELO	HOLT
ATLAS	HUGO
AXEL	IGOR
BART	IVOR
BOONE	JOCK
BRAWLEY	KING
BROCK	KNOX
BRUNO	KNUTE
BRUTUS	MACK
BUBBA	MICK
BURR	OTTO
CLINT	PRIMO
CONAN	RAMBO
CORD	RIP
CURT	ROCCO
DALLAS	ROCK
DAX	ROCKY
DOLPH	ROD
DOMINIC	SAMSON
DUKE	THOR
FLINT	VITO
FORD	WOLF
GUS	ZOLTAN

MANLY NAMES

The names we call Manly have a Hallmark Father's Day card image: pipe, hunting dogs, golf clubs, the whole caboodle. They're the men's club of names, the Williams, Fredericks, and Josephs. If, in their proper form, some sound sort of, well, prissy, never fear; they come complete with Manly nicknames: Bill, Fred, Joe.

In terms of style, Manly names are on the upswing. With so many girls' names invading masculine turf—Whitney, Kyle, Alix, et al—boys' names are retreating to more exclusive ground. And many parents these days want their boys clearly to be boys, names and all.

Boys tend to fare well with these sturdy, classic names. No one ever gets teased for being called David, for instance, and no little Frank is ever mistaken for a girl on the basis of his name. The price you pay for this safety is that your son may not feel unique: There are relatively few classic boys' names and the selection is not all that inspired.

At the same time, the long craze for less traditional boys' names—the Jamies and Coreys, the Joshuas and Jasons of the last twenty years—freshens the sound of stalwarts like Henry and Fred. We may be moving back to the days when "every Tom, Dick, and Harry" was more than just a figure of speech.

Manly names

AL(L)AN/ALLEN	CHARLES
ALBERT	DANIEL
ALFRED	DAVID
ANDREW	DONALD
ANTHONY	DOUGLAS
ARTHUR	EARL
BERT/BURT	EDWARD
CARL	FRANK

FREDERICK	PATRICK
GEORGE	PAUL
GERALD	PETER
GORDON	PHIL(L)IP
HAROLD	RALPH
HARRY	RAYMOND
HARVEY	REX
HENRY	RICHARD
HOWARD	ROBERT
HUGH	ROGER
IVAN	RONALD
JACK	ROY
JAMES	RUSSELL
JOHN	SAMUEL
JOSEPH	STANLEY
KENNETH	STEPHEN
LAWRENCE	STUART/STEWART
LEO	THEODORE
LEONARD	THOMAS
LEWIS/LOUIS	VICTOR
MARK	VINCENT
MARTIN	WALTER
MICHAEL	WARREN
NEAL/NEIL	WILLIAM
NORMAN	

NEW MANLY NAMES

The last decade has seen the emergence of a new breed of names: names that bespeak a transformed masculine ideal—sensitized, enlightened, liberated from the manacles of machismo. Names for guys with Alan Alda eyes (and maybe a Dustin Hoffman nose), guys who shop and cook and Pamper their babies. Guys who cry.

Some of these New Manly names have already worn out their welcome, while others remain in vogue. Although a certain percentage, like Jonathan and Joshua, have traditional roots, for the most part these names have been in wide use only since the publication of *The Feminine Mystique.* This is not to suggest that they are feminine names. Most are unmistakably male, but neither are they muscle-bound, far right, or radical.

This group of names is for little boys who may still prefer to play with trucks and build with blocks, but who probably also have at least one anatomically correct doll on their shelves.

It reflects the imagination of the first generation of parents not to rely on the inert pool of traditional male names for their sons. In the mid-sixties, names like Eric, Scott, and yes, Jason started appearing on the list of the top fifty names for boys; by 1982, Jason was number five and a flock of other New Manly names from Justin to Joshua to Jonathan had unseated such old standbys as Arthur, Frederick, and Peter.

One reason for the wild rise in popularity of these New Manly names is that it became unfashionable to name a boy after his father or any other family patriarch. Patriarchy itself was unfashionable. Each child was seen as an individual, to be given a fresh and creative start in life.

While many of these names are still popular, as a group they are not as stylish as they were even a few years ago. Most of the boys' names on the So Far In They're Out list can be found here. Exceptions are many of the surname names, as well as newcomers like Rex, Clay, and Duncan that buck the Tom, Dick, and Harry tradition but haven't been as overused as the Jason and Joshua group.

Does all this mean that New Men are out of style? Well, yes and no. Although today's New Man has dried his tears, he still dries the dishes, and this firmed-up masculine image is reflected in the naming of boy babies.

New manly names

AARON
ABEL
ABNER
ADAM
AIDAN
ALEC
ALEX
ALEXANDER
AMOS
ANGUS
ANSON
ARI
ARLO
ASHER
AUSTIN
AVERY
BAILEY
BARNABY
BARTHOLOMEW
BEAU/BO
BEN
BENEDICT

BENJAMIN
BEVAN
BLAINE
BLAKE
BRADLEY
BRADY
BRANDON
BRENDAN
BRETT
BRODY
BRYANT
CALE
CALEB
CALVIN
CAMERON
CAMPBELL
CAREY
CARSON
CARTER
CARVER
CASE
CASEY

CHRISTIAN
CHRISTOPHER
CLANCY
CLAY
CLEMENT
CODY
COLIN
COREY
CURTIS
DALE
DALLAS
DALTON
DAMIEN/DAMIAN
DANE
DARCY
DASHIELL
DAVIS
DENVER
DEREK
DEVLIN
DEVON
DIRK
DONOVAN
DRAKE
DREW
DUNCAN
DUSTIN
DYLAN
EBEN
ELI
ELIA

ELIAS
ELIJAH
EL(L)IOT(T)
ELISHA
ELLIS
EMANUEL
EMMETT
EPHRAIM
ERIC
ETHAN
EVAN
EVERETT
EZRA
FABIAN
FORREST
FOSTER
GABRIEL
GARRETT
GIDEON
GRAHAM
GRAY/GREY
GREGORY
GRIFFIN
HALE
HUBBELL
HUNTER
IAN
ISAAC
ISAIAH
JACKSON
JACOB

JAKE	KENT
JAMIE	KERRY
JARED	KIM
JARRETT	KIRK
JARVIS	KYLE
JASON	LANDON
JASPER	LANE
JED	LEMUEL
JEDIDIAH	LEVI
JEFFREY	LIAM
JEREMIAH	LINCOLN
JEREMIAS	LINUS
JEREMY	LIONEL
JESSE	LOREN
JODY	LORNE
JON	LUCAS
JONAH	LUCIAN
JONAS	LUCIUS
JONATHAN	LUKE
JORDAN	MACKENZIE
JOSH	MALACHI/
JOSHUA	MALACHY
JOSIAH	MALCOLM
JUD(D)	MARC
JUDE	MARCO
JULIAN	MARCUS
JUSTIN	MASON
KAI	MATTHEW
KEIL	MATTHIAS
KEIR	MAX
KELLY	MAXWELL

MICAH	RYAN
MILO	SAM
MORGAN	SAUL
MOSES	SAWYER
NATHAN	SEAN/SHAWN
NATHANIEL	SEBASTIAN
NED	SETH
NICHOLAS	SHANE
NOAH	SILAS
NOEL	SIMON
NOLAN	SOLOMON
OLIVER	TAYLOR
OMAR	THADDEUS
OTIS	THEO
OWEN	TIMOTHY
QUENTIN	TOBIAH
QUINN	TOBIAS
RAPHAEL	TRACY
REDMOND	TRAVIS
REED	TREVOR
RENO	TRISTAN
REO	TYLER
REUBEN	WALKER
RILEY	WEBB
ROBINSON	WILEY/WYLIE
ROLLO	WILL
RORY	WYATT
ROSS	WYNN
ROWAN	YALE
RUFUS	ZACHARIAH/S
RUPERT	ZACHARY

ZACK/ZAK	ZED
ZANE	ZEKE

WIMPY NAMES

No matter how sensitive you want your son to be, you surely don't want to brand him as a wimp. You don't want to give him a name that will get him picked last for every team, shunned in every game of spin the bottle, turned down for every blind date.

Unfair as it may seem, the Selwyns and Percys and Egberts of this world tend to meet one of two terrible fates. Either they knuckle under to their names, and *become* Selwyns or Percys or Egberts; or they bust their gonads proving that, despite the wimpy label, they're really Rods or Brunos or Rambos.

We have been conservative in devising this list. We have avoided borderline wimpy names, and concentrated on the hard (soft?) core group. What relegates a name to terminal wimpdom?

Once-ambisexual names now used almost exclusively for girls qualify: Lynn or Courtney, for example. A feminine sound, like the sibilant Percy or Sylvester, can push a name into the wimp category. And any name ending in "-bert" (Hubert, Egbert, Wilbert) or "-ville" (Melville, Orville) or "-wyn/vin" (Selwyn, Melvin) almost automatically triggers a wimp response in the modern ear.

This brings up a salient point for any of you out there with decidedly nonwimpy uncles or fathers named Bernard or Melvin. Perceptions of wimpiness tend to change over generations. As Russell Baker points out (see page 173), Jason was once one of the biggest wimp names going. And a name that seems perfectly substantial for a fifty-year-old man can suddenly go limp when applied to a newborn baby of today.

Obviously, this list is intended more as a warning than a guide-post. If you're determined to go ahead with one of these names, maybe you should be prepared to spend your old age introducing Percy as "My son, the butterfly collector" or "My son, the merce-nary guerrilla." Tough choice, eh?

Wimpy names

AINSLEY
ALGERNON
ALOYSIUS
ALVIN
AMBERT
ARNOLD
BEAUREGARD
BENTLEY
BERNARD
BERTRAM
BLAIR
BROOKE
BROOKS
BRUCE
BURTON
CARLTON
CARROLL
CECIL
CEDRIC
CHARLTON
CLARENCE
CONWAY
CORNELIUS
COURTNEY
CYRIL
DABNEY
DELMORE
DEWEY
DURWOOD
DWIGHT
EDGAR
EGBERT
ELBERT
ELLSWORTH
ELMER
ELROY
EUGENE
FARLEY
FERDINAND
FLOYD
FRANCIS
GALE
GAYLORD
GOMER

HARMON	MILTON
HERBERT	MONROE
HERMAN	MORTIMER
HORACE	MURRAY
HUBERT	MYRON
HUMPHREY	NORBERT
HYMAN	ORVILLE
IRA	OSBERT
IRVING	OSWALD
IRWIN	PERCIVAL
JULIUS	PERCY
KERWIN	REGINALD
LANCE	RODNEY
LEON	ROOSEVELT
LESLIE	SANFORD
LESTER	SELWYN
LYNDON	SEYMOUR
LYNN	SHELDON
MANFRED	SHERMAN
MARION	SHERWOOD
MARLON	SYLVESTER
MARMADUKE	THURMAN
MARVIN	VANCE
MAURICE	VERNON
MAYNARD	VIRGIL
MELVILLE	WENDELL
MELVIN	WESLEY
MERLE	WILBERT
MERLIN	WILBUR
MERTON	WILFRED
MERVYN	

Don't Pick a Fight with Bruce

A wimpy name does not necessarily a wimpy boy make. In fact, the world is full of Bruces, Arnolds, and Sylvesters we wouldn't want to meet in a dark alley. Maybe these guys became supermacho in reaction to their anemic names, or maybe they would have overdeveloped biceps even if their names were Brawley or Flint. Here, a list of famous tough guys with anything but tough names.

ARNOLD
  Schwarzenegger
BROOKS Robinson
BRUCE Jenner
BRUCE Lee
BRUCE Springsteen
BRUCE Weitz
CARLTON Fisk
CARROLL O'Connor
CECIL Cooper
CHARLTON Heston
CLARENCE Clemons
DWIGHT Gooden
ELROY Hirsch
ELVIS Presley
ERNEST Borgnine
ERNEST Hemingway
FRAN Tarkenton
GALE Sayers

GAYLORD Perry
JULIUS Erving
HARMON Killebrew
HERSCHEL Walker
HUMPHREY Bogart
LEON Spinks
LYNDON Johnson
LYNN Swann
MARION Motley
MARLON Brando
MARVIN Hagler
MEL Gibson
MERLE Haggard
MERLIN Olsen
REGGIE Jackson
ROOSEVELT
  (ROSIE) Greer
SYLVESTER Stallone
THURMAN Munson

What Jason Was

> When I was a child, only the most sadistic parents named their children Jason. . . . Like Percy and Horace, Jasons existed only to be beaten in the schoolyard by classmates named Spike and Butch.
>
> —Russell Baker, "A Name for All Seasons," Sunday Observer, *The New York Times,* 1984

BEACH BOYS

In the late fifties and early sixties, no names were cooler than Gary, Glenn, and Greg. They were the personification of surfer machismo. Now, however, these Beach Boy names have lost their muscle. They are too old to be new men, too young to be manly, too soft to be macho, and too firm to be truly wimpy. This group of masculine nomads includes:

BRAD	GLENN
BRIAN	GREG
CHAD	KEITH
CRAIG	KEVIN
DARREN	RICK
DARRYL	SCOTT
DEAN	TODD
DENNIS	TROY
DUANE/DWAYNE	WAYNE
GARY	

At five, Marlon had an angelic face and a pugnacious nature, developed as a defense against neighborhood bullies who taunted him about his fancy-sounding name.

—*The Star,* November 10, 1987, excerpted from *Brando: A Biography in Photographs,* by Christopher Nickens

"Do they mean Bruce Springsteen? Bruce Willis? Bruce really seems to be the in name these days."

—Bruce Boxleitner on TV talk show when shown two girls wearing I Love Bruce buttons

AMBISEXUAL NAMES

The trend over the past twenty years has increasingly been to bestow ambisexual names upon girls rather than boys. And once a name moves from the male province into the female, there's usually no going back.

There have been a number of transsexual shifts in the history of nomenclature. Alice, Anne, Crystal, Emma, Esmé, Evelyn, Florence, Jocelyn, Kimberly, Lucy, and Maud all were originally male names. Christian was a feminine name in the Middle Ages, as was Douglas in the seventeenth century and Clarence in the eighteenth. A king of East Anglia in the seventh century was named Anna.

In the sixties, it was more usual to find a boy with an ambisexual name than it is now. The big trend in that consciousness-raising time was toward cute nicknames that sounded just as right for boys as for girls: Jody, Toby, Jamie. This continued in the seventies with ambisexual nicknames that were short for more sexually distinct proper names. There were plenty of Chrises, Nickys, and Alexes around, but on their birth certificates they were Christopher or Christine, Nicholas or Nicole, Alexander or Alexandra.

More recently we've moved back to ambisexual proper names without nicknames, but, as detailed in the Androgynous Executive list in the What's Hot section, these are used more and more for girls rather than boys. While a carriage bearing an Alexis, Blair, or Jordan may still hold a boy, it's more likely that the blanket in it will be pink and the baby will be female.

In the vanguard of style, parents are even considering traditionally masculine names for their daughters. One couple we know—a television producer and a theatrical lawyer—said that if their child was a girl, they would name her George. Fortunately, they had a boy.

We've arranged the following list of Ambisexual names from those that are at the moment used almost exclusively for girls to those used primarily for boys. When a name had variant spellings for boys and girls, we've included both, but with nickname names like Ricky and Terry, we've listed only the ambi y ending.

This list can be a help in determining the current gender standing of a name. But, be warned: We predict that by the turn of the next century many of the names in the 50 percent range will have moved into the feminine dominion, and that names like Jordan and Perry and Daryl may well be considered about as appropriate for a boy as, say, Sue.

90 percent feminine

ALLIE/ALLY   CAROL (f);
ANDREA   CARROLL (m)

CHRISTIE/
  CHRISTY
CLAIRE (f); CLARE
  (f,m)
COURTNEY
EVELYN
GAIL (f); GALE (f,m)
HA(Y)LEY
HIL(L)ARY

JOYCE
KAY
LACEY
LAURIE
LYNN
MARIAN/MARION
PA(I)GE
SHANNON
TRACY

75 percent feminine

ALEXIS
ASHLEY
BLAIR
BROOKE
BRYN
DANA
JAN
KELLY
KELSEY
KERRY
KIM
KIT

LAUREN (f);
  LOREN (f,m)
LESLIE/LESLEY
LINDSAY/LINDSEY
MALLORY
MEREDITH
MERRILL
PATSY
ROBIN
SACHA/SASHA
SHELL(E)Y
STACY
WHITNEY

50/50

ALEX	JESS(I)E
ALI	JODY
ANGEL	JORDAN
BO	KAI
BRETT	LANE
CAREY	LEE (f,m); LEIGH (f)
CASEY	MACKENZIE
CASS	MICKEY
CHRIS	MORGAN
COREY	NICKY
DALE	PAT
DARCY	PAYTON
DEVON	RICKY
DORIAN	SHAWN (f,m); SEAN
EVAN	(m)
FRANCES (f);	STORM
FRANCIS (m)	SYDNEY (f,m);
GERRY (f,m); JERRY	SIDNEY (m)
(f,m)	TERRY
HOLLIS	TOBY
JAMIE	WALLIS (f,m);
JEAN (f); GENE (f,m)	WALLACE (m)

75 percent male

BAILEY	CAMERON
BLAKE	DARIN/DARREN

DAR(R)YL
DREW
DYLAN
ELLERY
EMLYN
KEIL
KIRBY
KYLE
NEVADA
NOEL (m,f); NOELLE (f)
NORRIS
PALMER
PARKER
PERRY
PORTER
QUINN

RANDY
RAY (m,f); RAE (f)
REED
REGAN
RORY
SAM
SCHUYLER
SHELBY
SIERRA
SLOAN
TAYLOR
TYLER
VALENTINE
WALKER
WYNN
YAEL

90 percent masculine

ADDISON
AIDAN
AL(L)AN/ALLEN (m);
    ALLYN (m,f)
BROWN
CHRISTOPHER
CLAUDE
DALLAS

GARY
GEORGE
GLENN
MEL
MICHAEL
SETH
SHANE
ZANE

No Boys Named Maria

In 1932, the Supreme Court of Czechoslovakia ruled that Maria would no longer be allowed as a name for male children. The tribunal decided that a given name must clearly denote an individual's sex.

"By the time Jamie goes to college, it's probably going to cost about $29,000 a year. Either I'd better make some smart decisions or else she'd better learn to play football."

—Citibank TV commercial

TRADITION

"Hakeem?" "Here." "Liam?" "Here." "Sarita?" "Here." Attendance-taking time at any self-respecting preschool these days will tell you that tradition as an influence on naming is back with a vengeance.

You, like many parents, may be looking into your own familial history—canvassing the names of grandparents, great-aunts, and uncles—to come up with a name for your child that reflects your cultural heritage. You may be considering a family surname for your baby's middle or even first name, whether your child is a boy or a girl. And if a suitable name can't be plucked from your own family tree, you may find yourself wandering into other orchards in search of a seasoned name, a name with substance.

To give you a perspective on the past, we offer here a history of this century's naming trends, the fashions and fads that typified each decade. Also here is a guide to nicknames: the rise and fall in popularity of a range of abbreviated forms, including some no longer used versions—Daisy for Margaret, for example, or Hobbin for Robert—you may find worth consideration.

You may want to incorporate tradition in your child's name by choosing one that reflects your ethnic heritage. Let's say you're Irish, and you'd like to explore options beyond the obvious Shannon, Kevin, and cousins. In one section here you'll learn that Brett, Tracy, Darren, and Troy, among others, would all be authentically Irish choices, even though you may have believed otherwise. Another chapter will give you some exotic names—how do Annora, Juno, Curran, or Eamon strike you?—popular in Ireland but rarely heard here, along with similar lists for other cultural backgrounds, from Hebrew to Italian to Hungarian. And if you're looking for a name to reflect black heritage, included here are lists of Arabic and African names.

If your hope is to come up with a name that connects to the religious traditions of your family, you may want to consult the list of unexpected saints' names—and take this book to the baptism to convince the priest there really is a Saint Benno. Also here is a guide to Jewish naming traditions, including examples of how the first-initial practice and secular trends have combined to bring naming patterns full circle.

Our focus on tradition narrows in the chapter called Family Ties. Are you and your spouse wrestling over name choices? Here's why, plus tips to help you come to a compatible decision. If you're thinking of making your son a junior, you'll find the pros and cons here. Also here is a guide to sibling names—for first-time parents, too! And finally, we offer a primer on living with your ultimate choice of name.

Here, then, to Tradition, the fourth important factor in choosing the right name for your child.

AMERICAN
NOMENCLATURE

TRADITION IN PROGRESS

There are two currents of tradition in American names.

One is really an English tradition, names brought over by the Pilgrims and handed down from generation to generation, from century to century. Mary, Ann, Catherine, and Elizabeth; John, James, Charles, Joseph, Robert, William, and Edward were as well used here in 1750 as they were in 1900 and as they are today, but are no more uniquely American than, say, an *Oxford Dictionary*.

A naming tradition America could call its own didn't really blossom until 1920. By that time, when our parents' parents bobbed their hair and shaved their mustaches, put in a phone, and searched for modern baby names, there were places to look: at the marquee of the new movie theatre down the block, to the voices on the radio now dominating the living room, or at the neighbors who just arrived from County Cork.

American tradition is one part history and three parts experimentation, fashion, and progress—with a strong dash of folly. To get a true picture, you have to consider chili dogs along with apple pie, Groundhog Day as well as the Fourth of July, Mickey along with Michael.

Here, a look at the naming tradition we've just begun to create.

The 64 Percent Solution

It has been estimated that in fourteenth-century England 64 percent of all male children were given one of the following five names:

HENRY
JOHN
ROBERT
WILLIAM
RICHARD

Today, by contrast, roughly the same proportion of boys receive names ranked in the top fifty.

The 1920s and 1930s: Freckles, France, and Hollywood

The hottest trend in the 1920s and early 1930s was freckle-faced names for girls and boys, Our Gang comedy names that came complete with button noses, big ears, and overbites. A lot of these were nicknames for perennial favorites—Billy or Willie for William, for example, or Margie, Maggie, and Peggy for Margaret—but others were proper names you just don't hear much anymore:

G I R L S

BETSY	PATSY
BINNIE	PEGGY
DOLLY	PENNY
GWEN	POLLY
KATHLEEN	SALLY
KITTY	TRUDY
MARY ANN	WINNIE

B O Y S

BARNEY	FRANKLIN
CALVIN	HAL
CHESTER	HOMER
CLEM	MICKEY
DEXTER	NED
ELMER	WILBUR
EUGENE	WILLIS

At the same time, several names, often those popularized by stars, were new arrivals on the best-seller list. For girls: Alice, Barbara, Betty, Jean, Marion, Myrna, Patricia, Shirley, and Virginia; for boys, Arthur, Clarence, Donald, Harry, Henry, Richard, and Thomas.

Other female fads of the period included names of the months (April, May, and June); names ending in the letter *s* (Phyllis, Frances, Doris, Lois, Iris); and names ending in *-een* or *-ine*—Irish ones like Eileen, Maureen, Pegeen, Noreen, Kathleen, and Colleen, or more Gallic specimens like Jacqueline, Maxine, Arlene, Nadine, Pauline, and Marlene, which followed in the wake of such earlier favorites as Irene, Geraldine, and Josephine. Even more fashionably French were Annette, Claudette, Paulette, Georgette, Jeanette, and Nanette, not to mention Rochelle, Estelle, and Isabel.

Diamond-Studded Names

What were the most glittery names of 1927? Or at least what did the copywriters of the Sears, Roebuck catalog of that year think would appear as such to their constituency when they decided to give girls' names to the various models of "Genuine Brilliant Diamond Rings"?

They were:

ABBIE	INEZ
ALICE	IRENE
ANGELA	JANET
ANNA MAY	KATHRYN
ANNETTE	LORRAINE MAY
BETTY JANE	LYDIA
BEULAH	MARILYN
CLARICE	MILDRED
ELAINE	MINERVA
ELEANOR	PAULINE
FLORENCE	RUTH
GENEVIEVE	VIOLA
HONORA	

The 1930s and 1940s: Hi Mom! Hi Dad! I'm home!

During the mid-thirties through the forties, names like Dorothy, Anne, Shirley, Ruth, George, Frank, Edward, and Clarence fell off the top ten, to be replaced by Carol, Judith, Joan, Linda, Ronald, and David. Other new names were moving in as well—"sophisticated" names for kids whose parents envisioned them triumphing over the Depression and growing up to use cigarette holders, wear glamorous evening clothes, and live in Hollywood-inspired mansions. Television was still in its infancy, so no one could foresee that these would become the sitcom mom and dad names of the next generation:

G I R L S

ANITA	LORRAINE
AUDREY	LYNN
BEVERLY	MARILYN
BRENDA	MARJORIE
CYNTHIA	NANCY
DEBORAH	NATALIE
DIANE	PAMELA
ELAINE	RENÉE
ELLEN	ROBERTA
GAIL	SANDRA
JANE	SHEILA
JANET	SUSAN
JOANNE	

B O Y S

AL(L)AN/ALLEN	MICHAEL
BERT/BURT	NEIL/NEAL
CHRISTOPHER	NORMAN
EL(L)IOT(T)	PAUL
GERALD	PETER
GILBERT	PHIL(L)IP
HAROLD	ROGER
HARVEY	RUSSELL
HERBERT	STANLEY
HOWARD	STEPHEN
JOEL	WALTER
LAWRENCE	WARREN
MARTIN	

The 1950s: Ranch houses and barbeques

The postwar baby boom moving into the fifties spawned a whole new generation of cuter, younger, glossier names, names for kids who would play with Tiny Tears dolls and watch Captain Kangaroo, oblivious to the hard times just past. These names reflected a collective lust for a new way of life, the good life in the suburbs. Linda jumped from number ten to number one in popularity and Karen appeared out of nowhere to take the tenth spot. Michael, a Biblical name that had been out of favor for over a hundred years, catapulted to number two. Other newly popular names in the fifties, many of which remained in vogue through the Kennedy administration, were:

G I R L S

AMY	JANICE
CHARLENE	JULIE
CHERYL	LISA
CHRISTINE	MICHELLE
DARLENE	ROBIN
DENISE	SHARON
DONNA	TERRY
HEIDI	TINA
HOLLY	WENDY

B O Y S

ANDREW	JEFFREY
ANTHONY	KENNETH
BRIAN	KEVIN
BRUCE	LEE
CRAIG	MARK
DEAN	PATRICK
DENNIS	SCOTT
DOUGLAS	TERRY
ERIC	TIMOTHY
GARY	TODD
GREGORY	

The 1960s: Do your own thing

In the sixties and early seventies, as men grew their hair to their shoulders and women abandoned their bras, Karens and Craigs gave way to Caryns and Chastitys, Kellys and Clouds. In deference to the new credo of "do your own thing," new names were invented, familiar forms of old names became perfectly acceptable, and the spelling of traditional names became a contest of creativity. The ultimate trendy name of the sexually liberated sixties and early seventies was actually a relaxed nickname name, preferably ambigender. We saw a lot of the following:

CANDY	MANDY
CARRIE/CAREY	MARCY
CASEY	MARNIE
CINDY	MINDY
COREY	RICKI/RICKY
JAMIE	SHARI
JESSIE/JESSE	SHELL(E)Y
JODY	SHERRY
JONI/JON	STACY
KELLY	TAMMY
KERRY	TAWNY
KIM	TRACY
LORI	

Even more revolutionary were such invented hippie names as:

AMERICA	CHINA
ASIA	CLOUD
BREEZE	DAKOTA
CHE	DUNE

ECHO	REBEL
FOREST	RIVER
FREE	SEASON
GYPSY	SENECA
HARMONY	SEQUOIAH
LEAF	SIERRA
LIBERTY	SKY
LIGHT	SPRING
LOVE	STAR
MORNING	STARSHINE
OCEAN	SUMMER
PEACE	SUNSHINE
PHOENIX	TRUE
RAIN	WELCOME
RAINBOW	WILLOW

The Names, They Are A-Changing

Now that lovebeads and elephant bells are nostalgia items, many of the flower children's children are trading in their hippie names for more mainstream ones. Zowie Bowie, for instance, son of David Bowie, now calls himself Joey. Free, born to David Carradine and Barbara Hershey when she was calling herself Barbara Seagull, has changed his name to Tom. And Susan St. James, who named her first two children Harmony and Sunshine, called her sons born in the eighties Charlie and William.

As the children born in the sixties and early seventies come of age, however, we'll be hearing more from those who are standing by the names given them by their idealistic parents. One already notable example is River Phoenix,

who came to prominence in the 1986 film, *Stand by Me.*
River's sisters are named Rainbow, Liberty, and Summer,
Joy, and his brother is named Leaf. The father of the Phoe-
nix family is named—what else?—John.

The 1970s: Ahead to the past

The mid-seventies saw the beginnings of a reawakening of patrio-
tism, but this tentative romance was with a pre-Watergate, pre-
Vietnam, pre-Bomb, pre-Depression, pre-Industrial Revolution
America—way back to the old West. Fifty years after the birth of
a uniquely American naming tradition, we finally summoned the
confidence to delve back into our country's own past, launching a
nation of little urban cowboys and their pioneer-women sisters
named:

G I R L S

AMY	JENNY
ANNIE	JESSIE
BECKY	MOLLY

B O Y S

ETHAN	JOSH
JASON	LUKE
JED	SHANE
JESSE	ZANE

Also, Biblical names like Aaron, Adam, Benjamin, Jacob, Jonathan, Rachel, Rebecca, Sarah, and Samuel were born again, even if the parents choosing them weren't.

Those who couldn't or didn't want to reach back to the frontier or the Bible for their roots looked to their own or other people's ethnic backgrounds for inspiration (see Roots, page 221). Names derived from the Irish or French became particularly popular, even for parents who weren't Irish or French. Thus were born thousands of Brians, Dylans, Erins, Kellys, Kevins, Megans, Ryans, Seans, Shannons, and Taras. For girls, the French twist was the rage, with names such as Danielle, Michelle (given a big boost by the Beatles song), and Nicole.

Other little girls were liberated from female stereotypes with names previously reserved for effete upper-class gentlemen: Ashley, Blake, Brooke, Courtney, Kimberly, Lindsay, and Whitney. Similar in tone, although they were always girls' names, are Hayley (as in Mills) and Tiffany (yes: a Charlie's Angel).

At the opposite end of the scale is a group of girls' names as purely feminine as a lavender sachet. These are the wildly popular Victorian valentine names, which include Alexandra, Alyssa (in all its variant spellings), Amanda, Jennifer, Jessica, Samantha, Melissa, Vanessa, and Victoria. Their male counterparts are Alexander, Brett, Justin, and Nicholas.

Today, while many of the names that became popular in the 1970s are still widely used, their fashion status is fading. But their legacy is important: They reflect renewed ties with tradition, the rejuvenation of forgotten classics, a closer bond between names and ethnic or religious heritage. These issues are important to many of today's parents, whose name choices will influence the American traditions of tomorrow.

THE HUNDRED-YEAR CYCLE

When was the last time that names like Alexander, Benjamin, Amanda, and Gregory were in vogue? A startling number of the names that sound fresh and appealing to us today were favored by the new parents of a hundred years ago. Appearing in the top-fifty lists a century ago were:

G I R L S

ANNIE	LAURA
CARRIE	LILLIE
CHARLOTTE	LUCY
ELIZABETH	REBECCA
EMILY	SARA(H)
JENNIE	SOPHIA
KATHERINE	

B O Y S

ALEXANDER	HENRY
ANDREW	JACOB
BENJAMIN	JAMES
CHARLES	JOHN
DAVID	SAMUEL
EDWARD	WILLIAM
HARRY	

Other names that didn't make the top fifty but were in fashion a hundred years ago, and are back in style now, include:

G I R L S

AMANDA	LOUISE
CHRISTINA	MADELINE
CLAIRE	MAGGIE
DAISY	OLIVIA
JULIA	POLLY
LEAH	RACHEL

B O Y S

AARON	JOSHUA
ADAM	LUKE
ANTHONY	MAX
BEN	NATHAN
ERIC	NOAH
GREGORY	PATRICK
JESSE	SETH
JONAH	TIMOTHY
JONATHAN	

CATHERINE, KATHARINE, AND KATHRYNNE

You've always loved the name Catherine. But you want your Catherine to be unique; different from all the others in the world, so you decide to spell it Kathrynne.

You see the first signs of trouble while still in the hospital, where you are asked to spell the name eleven times. This is followed by similar requests from friends, parents, in-laws, aunts, and cousins, who nevertheless send cards and little pink panda bears addressed to Katharine, Katherine, Kathryn, Kathrinne, and Kathy Lynn.

Creative naming was one of the least felicitous minirevolutions to take place during the Age of Aquarius, when suddenly there was a nonaggressive army of Alicias, Alishas, Alysias, Alisas, Alyssas, Elissas, Elyssas, Ilysas, and Ilyssas peacefully coexisting in the park with Arons, Jaysens, Kristoffers, and Jimis.

While the use of unconventional spellings is no longer epidemic, the practice continues. Recent aberrations noted on birth announcements have included Kassie, Kacie, Kaitlin, Crystine, Holli, Malissa, Megean, Ryann, Jayme, and Jaimie.

Many of these children will grow up surrounded by people who think they don't know how to spell their own names, or that their parents (this means you) were simply ignorant. Poor Megean will have to spend countless hours explaining whether her name rhymes with Pegeen, Regan, or leg in, and many more hours correcting all the people who spell her name wrong by spelling it right.

A different issue arises when a name has bona fide variant spellings, each of which is widely used and accepted. Once again, Catherine is a case in point: the C spelling is originally French and commonly used in Britain; Katherine is the most common form in the United States and Canada; Katharine is derived from the name's Roman version and also well used here; and Kathryn is a spelling used since the turn of the century and popularized in the 1940s by the actress Kathryn (b. Zelma) Grayson.

Other names with more than one well-accepted spelling include Ann/Anne, Sara/Sarah, Alison/Allison, Stuart/Stewart, Teresa/Theresa, Alan/Allan/Allen, Geoffrey/Jeffrey, Lee/Leigh, Philip/Phillip, and Stephen/Steven.

While all these names are pronounced the same whatever the spelling, which form you choose seems to alter the name in subtle ways. Katherine, for instance, seems somewhat hipper than Catherine, which has a more feminine and gently old-fashioned connotation. Ann seems more no-nonsense than Anne, Leigh more delicate than Lee, Geoffrey more buttoned-up than Jeffrey.

When there is more than one correct spelling of a name, let your own feelings on the image each conjures up be your guide. Catherine, Katherine, Katharine, and Kathryn are all perfectly correct choices, and all a far sight better than (please don't) Kathrynne.

I kept wishing for some poor people, some important characters much older, or younger, than these nummies, someone whose name weren't Garrett, or Gaye, or Kyle, or Renée, or Drew.

—Thomas R. Edwards, review of *Where You'll Find Me and Other Stories* by Ann Beattie, *The New York Times Book Review*, October 12, 1986

WHY JENNIFER AND JASON?

How did Jennifer and Jason become popular to the point of infamy?

Jennifer, consistently the number-one name in most states since the early seventies, was an overnight success largely inspired by the doomed heroine Jenny in *Love Story*. But while the book—and later the movie—may have launched the name, a perfect fit with the spirit of the times sustained it.

Jennifer was a name with something for almost everyone. For down-home, back-to-the-land types, it had the cowgirlish nickname Jenny. Jenny, by itself, was also a Grandma and Grandpa name (foreshadowing today's popularity of Max, Sam, et al) shared by grandmas who hailed from places as diverse as Minsk and Mayo. And Jennifer in its full glory had a romantically feminine Victorian flavor as well as a euphonic, air-brushed quality—both in vogue in the seventies.

Jason, on the other hand, never quite made it to number one: More traditional boys' names like Michael and Christopher claimed that honor. But Jason is the quintessential trendy boy's name of the seventies—newfangled but old-fashioned, with roots in both the Old West and the Old Testament. Again, many different types of parents—from Jews to born-again Christians, from *Ms.* magazine readers to Clint Eastwood fans—could, and did, find a reason to name their sons Jason.

Jason's and even Jennifer's star is on the wane now. While Jennifer is a name that still has mass appeal, many parents are turning away from it because of the sheer volume of little Jennifers. But the names they're favoring instead—notably Ashley, Amanda, and Jessica—have such a similar flavor that they seem like consolation prizes. Jason is suffering from a more rapid decline, losing out to classic upstarts like Andrew, Daniel, and Nicholas.

A GRAND OLD NAME

For three centuries, from the days when Mary was dressed in sober gowns of Puritan gray, to the days when she wore a bustle, to the days when she bobbed her hair, her name was always the most popular. The Greek and New Testament version of the Hebrew Miriam, Mary was considered too holy for mortal use until the twelfth century; by the sixteenth, it had become the most frequently used girl's name, a position it held until 1950.

That year, Linda made headline news by toppling Mary from the number-one spot. Mary continued on a downward slide, dropping to number fifteen in 1970 and thirty-four in 1983. Even the current resurgence in classic names has not boosted Mary back into favor.

The problem may be that Mary has become more of an icon than a name. Besides its association with the Blessed Virgin, it has a persistently ethnic ring and a fade-into-the-woodwork quality. Three hundred years of popularity have turned it into a generic term.

The name Mary remains fascinating, however, because of all the ways it has been used and the variations it has spawned. Some Catholic parents, for instance, use it as a token first name, followed by a sprightlier middle name by which their child is known. All four female members of the Fisher quintuplets, born in 1963, were named Mary: Mary Ann, Mary Magdalene, Mary Catherine, and Mary Margaret. And two of Robert and Ethel Kennedy's four daughters are named Mary—Mary Courtney and Mary Kerry—but called only by their middle names. The idea is that, since a Catholic child must carry a saint's name, Mary is sanctified enough to cover all bases, including a "heathen" middle name.

More often, when Mary is linked with another name, both are used. This "Mary-plus" trend reached its height in the 1940s and continued into the fifties, with variations ranging from the sedate Mary Ann and Mary Frances to the hep Mary Sue and Mary Jo to the oh-so-cute twins named Mary Pride and, yes, Mary Joy.

If the Mary-plus fad has (thankfully) gone the way of poodle skirts, derivations of the name Mary have become somewhat more common in this country. Those used here include:

MARA	MARIAH
MARIA	MARIAN/MARION

MARIAN(N)A   MARIS(S)A
MARIANNE   MARLA
MARIBEL   MARLENE
MARIE   MARLO
MARIEL   MARYA
MARIETTA   MAURA
MARIETTE   MAUREEN
MARILEE   MAY
MARILYN   MERRY
MARIN   MIA
MARINA   MOLLY
MARIS

The name Mary has no fewer foreign variations, which include the Irish Maire and Moira, the French Manette, the British Marigold, and—back to the source—the Hebrew Marilla.

VARIATIONS ON A THEME

When we were growing up, you weren't cool if you didn't have a nickname. Patti, Judy, Billy, and Bobby would rather have traded in their Beatle boots than be known to the world as Patricia, Judith, William, and Robert. The epitome of keen was to have a name that nobody could formalize when they were mad at you, a name that was a nickname: Jamie, Jody, Ricki.

President Carter changed all that. When he signed in as Jimmy in 1976, many people felt buoyed by the symbolism: He was a common man, leader of a nation of Toms and Daves, Kathys and Debbies. Later, the general sentiment was that a Jimmy wasn't up to the job: We needed a James to take us into the eighties. We elected Ronald—Ronnie only to his intimates and his enemies—Reagan and readopted the names on our own birth certificates, becoming Jameses and Deborahs and Richards ourselves.

Now, we're also favoring unabbreviated forms for our children: Today's little Elizabeth is more likely to lisp through all four syllables of her name than to introduce herself as Beth, Betsy, Libby, Lizzie, or any of the other possibilities.

This no-nickname trend has intensified what has long been a concern for parents: how to prevent other people from using the wrong—or any—nickname. Some parents solve this dilemma by choosing a name with no common diminutive: Claire, for example, or Ethan. Others may avoid a name they like because it has a nickname they don't care for. Two sets of parents we know decided against Susannah because they couldn't bear Susie or Sue; another couple who wanted to name their son Edward and call him Ned got cold feet at the possibility of raising an Eddie.

Nicknaming began in medieval England, where there were so few Christian names in general usage that it was not unusual for two children in a family to have the same name. The only way to distinguish the two Jameses was for one to be Jamey, the other Jem.

Many proper names that have remained in common use since that time have accumulated a procession of nicknames that reflect changing styles. Some of these nicknames were popular at one point and then died out: Tetty for Elizabeth, Sukey for Susan, and Hob for Robert, for example. Others have regularly moved in and out of fashion.

Here, with the range of nicknames used over time—arranged in order from the earliest to the most recent favorites—are some examples:

E L I Z A B E T H

BESS
ELIZA
BET
TETTY
TETSY
LIZZIE
BETH
BESSIE
LIBBY
BETTY
BETTE
BETSY
LISA
LIZ
LIZA
BETH
LIZZIE
BESS

C A T H E R I N E /
K A T H E R I N E

KITTY
KATE
CAT
KITTY
CASSY
KIT
KAY
CATHY/KATHY
KATIE
KATE

M A R G A R E T

DAISY
MAISIE
MAGGIE
MAG
MEG
MADGE
PEGGY
PEG
MARGE
MARGIE
MARGY
MAGGIE
MEG

MARY

MAL
MALLY
MOLL
MOLLY
POLLY
MAY
MINNIE
MAMIE
MAME
MITZI
MIMI

LAURA

LOLLY
LOW
LOR
LAURIE
LORI

BARBARA

BAB
BABBY
BABS
BOBBIE/BOBBY
BARB
BARBIE

PATRICIA

PAT
PATTY
PATSY
PAT
PATTY
PATTI
TRICIA
TRISH

WILLIAM

WILL
WILLY
WILLIE
BILL
BILLY
WILLIE
WILL

ROBERT	EDWARD
ROB	NED
HOB	TED
NOB	EDDY
DOB	ED
DOBBIN	EDDIE
ROBIN	TEDDY
BERT	NED
BOB	
BOBBY	**RICHARD**
ROBBIE	RICH
ROB	HITCH
	RICK
	HICK
	DICK
	RICHIE
	RICK
	RICKY

The ultimate fate of many of these series of nicknames is that those most widely used became names in their own right. Today, for instance, Molly and Kate are heard as often as their progenitors, Mary and Katherine. Other nicknames that have spun off into proper names bear little or no connection to their original forms. Nancy was once a nickname for Anne, for example, as was Sally for Sarah and Lisa for Elizabeth.

The Pete Pan Syndrome

A good case against calling your child by any kind of nickname can be found in the results of a study headed by Von Leirer, a psychologist at Human Cognition Research in Stanford, California. Students were asked to judge six fictitious people—two with formal names (like Peter), two with familiar ones (Pete), and two with "adolescent" nicknames (Petey). The Peters were rated as more conscientious, more emotionally stable, and more cultivated than the Petes and Peteys.

THE KOSHER CURVE

In general, except for the comparatively few people who are using Hebrew names for their children, there is no such thing as a "Jewish" first name anymore. The days when Molly Goldberg sticking her head out of her Bronx tenement window and calling down to her son Sammy meant immediate ethnic identification are long gone. These days, Sam's last name could just as readily be Gallagher and Mrs. Goldberg's son could be named Sean.

When today's Samuels and Benjamins are namesakes of Jewish great-grandpas, the phenomenon can be explained by an interesting theory concerning the cycles that occur in the naming patterns of immigrant families. According to the theory, first-generation immigrants typically renounce any clue to their ethnicity and so choose names for their children prevalent in general society. It is not until the third generation, or even later, that there is enough psychological distance for people to reembrace their ethnic heritage and incorporate it into their lives.

This is evidenced by the naming history of Jewish families in this country. The children of early immigrants turned to the most Anglo-Saxon sounding names they could find, lighting in particular upon aristocratic British surname-names like Stanley and Sheldon, Morton, Milton, and Melvin.

The following chart tracks some representative American Jewish given names from the turn of the century to the present.

ABE · ARTHUR · ALAN · ADAM · ABRAHAM

ANNIE · ANN · ANITA · AMY · ANNIE

BEN · BERNARD · BARRY · BRIAN · BEN

CLARA · CLAIRE · CAROL · CARRIE · CLAIRE

DORA · DOROTHY · DIANE · DEBBIE · DORIAN

FANNY · FRAN · FRANCES · FRANCESCA · FANNY

HARRY · HENRY · HARRIS · HARRISON · HENRY

ISAAC · IRVING · IRA · IAN · ISAAC

JAKE · JEROME · JAMES · JAY · JAKE

JENNY · JEAN · JANICE · JENNIFER · JENNA

LILY · LILIAN · LINDA · LORI · LILY

MAX · MARVIN · MITCHELL · MICHAEL · MAX

MOLLY · MARIAN · MARSHA · MARCY · MOLLY

NELLIE · NORMA · NANCY · NICOLE · NELL

RACHEL · RHODA · ROCHELLE · RICKI · RACHEL

ROSE · RUTH · RENÉE · RANDI · ROSIE

SADIE · SYLVIA · SUSAN · STACY · SADIE

SAM · SHELDON · STEVEN · SCOTT · SAM

SARAH · SELMA · SHEILA · SHELLY · SARAH

SOPHIE · SHIRLEY · SHARON · SHERRY · SOPHIE

Popular belief to the contrary, naming a Jewish child after a deceased relative is not mandated by any religious law or biblical text. Rather, the practice springs from a Jewish folklore belief that a person's name is his soul. In the Ashkenazic (Jews whose families originated in middle Europe) tradition, naming a child after a living relative could rob the relative of part of his soul and thus shorten his life. Today, even many nonreligious Jews carry a vestigial resistance toward naming a child after a living relative or friend.

This custom, however, is not practiced by Sephardic Jews (whose origins are in Southern Europe, North Africa, and the Middle East), who will name a child after a living relative. Traditionally, paternal grandparents are honored first, followed by maternal grandparents and then aunts and uncles. Infrequently, the child of a Sephardic family will even be named after a parent.

In both cultures, a baby usually isn't given the exact name of the person he is honoring, but a secular name with the same first letter as that person's Jewish or Hebrew name. The reason is not superstition, but simply that many parents don't like the ancestral name.

Double naming—giving a child both a mainstream and a religious name—began in the Middle Ages when the use of names taken from local languages had become so rampant that rabbis decreed that each Jewish boy be given a Hebrew (or otherwise sanctified) name at the time of his circumcision. Having two names soon became the custom for all Jewish babies; a child would have a sacred name, by which he would be called up to read the Torah, as well as a secular name for nonreligious purposes. First-generation American Jews would take their Hebrew names, say Avraham, and anglicize them to any English name beginning with the same initial, from the obvious Abraham to the more assimilated-sounding Arthur or Arnold.

The revival of the Hebrew language in Israel has prompted many American Jewish families to adopt traditional Hebrew names for their babies. Among the most popular are:

G I R L S

ALEEZA/ALIZA(H)	PUA(H)
ARIEL(LE)	SHIRA(H)
AVIVA(H)	TAMAR
CHAVA	TOVA(H)
DALYA/DALIA	TZURI(Y)A
ELAMA	VARDINA
LIORA/LEORA	YAEL
MICHAL	YAF(F)A
OFRA	YONA(H)
ORA(H)	

B O Y S

ADIN	GILAD
AMON/AMNON	MATAN
ARI	RAM
ASA	TAL
AVNER	URI
EITAN/EYTAN	UZI
ELAD	YITZHAR
ERAN	YOAV
GAD	ZOHAR
GIDEON	

FABIAN, PATRON SAINT OF ROCK AND ROLL, AND OTHER UNUSUAL, LIVELY, AND SURPRISING SAINTS' NAMES

If, because of tradition or religion, you want to give your child a saint's name, you don't have to settle for obvious choices like Anne, Cecelia, Anthony, or Joseph. Yes, there really is a Saint Fabian, as well as Saints Chad, Benno, Phoebe, Susanna, and Colette. What follows is a selective list of unexpected saints' names.

FEMALE

ADELA	ANTONIA
ADELAIDE	AQUILINA
AGATHA	ARIADNE
ALBINA	AUDREY
ANASTASIA	AURIA
ANGELA	AVA
ANGELINA	BEATRICE

BEATRIX	HYACINTH
BIBIANA	IDA
BRIDGET/BRIGID	ISABEL
CANDIDA	JANE
CHARITY	JOANNA
CHRISTINA	JULIA
CLARE	JULIANA
CLAUDIA	JUSTINA
CLEOPATRA	LELIA
CLOTILDA	LEWINA
COLETTE	LOUISA
COLUMBA	LUCRETIA
CRISPINA	LUCY
DARIA	LYDIA
DELPHINA	MARCELLA
DIANA	MARINA
DOROTHY	MARTINA
EBBA	MAURA
EDITH	MICHELINA
EMILY	ODILIA
EMMA	OLIVE
EUGENIA	PAULA
EULALIA	PETRONILLA
EVA	PHOEBE
FAITH	PRISCILLA
FELICITY	REGINA
FLORA	RITA
FRANCA	ROSALIA
GEMMA	SABINA
GENEVIEVE	SALOME
HEDDA	SANCHIA

SERAPHINA
SILVA
SUSANNA
TATIANA
THEA
THEODORA

THEODOSIA
VERENA
WINIFRED
ZENOBIA
ZITA

M A L E

AARON
ABEL
ABRAHAM
ADAM
ADOLF
ADRIAN
AIDAN
ALBERT
ALEXANDER
ALEXIS
AMBROSE
AMIAS
ANSELM
ARNOLD
ARTEMAS
BARDO
BARNABAS
BARTHOLOMEW
BASIL
BENEDICT
BENJAMIN

BENNO
BERTRAND
BLANE
BORIS
BRENDAN
BRUNO
CHAD
CLEMENT
CLETUS
COLMAN
CONAN
CONRAD
CORNELIUS
CRISPIN
CYPRIAN
CYRIL
DAMIAN
DANIEL
DECLAN
DONALD
DUNSTAN

EDMUND
EDWIN
ELIAS
EPHRAEM
ERASMUS
ERIC
ERNEST
EUGENE
EUSTACE
FABIAN
FELIX
FERGUS
FLAVIAN
FLORIAN
GERARD
GILBERT
GILES
GODFREY
GREGORY
GUNTHER
GUY
HERBERT
HILARY
HUBERT
HUGH
HUMBERT
ISAAC
ISIDORE
ISRAEL
JASON
JORDAN

JULIAN
JULIUS
KEVIN
KIERAN
KILIAN
LAMBERT
LEO
LEONARD
LINUS
LLOYD
LUCIAN
LUCIUS
MALACHY
MARIUS
MAXIMILIAN
MEL
MILO
MOSES
NORBERT
OSWALD
OTTO
OWEN
PIRAN
QUENTIN
RALPH
RAYMOND
ROCCO (Italian
    version of St. Roch)
RODERIC
RUFUS
RUPERT

SAMSON	TITUS
SEBASTIAN	VIRGIL
SILAS	WILFRED
SIMEON	WOLFGANG
SIMON	ZACHARY
SYLVESTER	ZENO
THEODORE	

Parents should choose suitable names for their children, avoiding such as are obscene, ridiculous or impious. It is advisable that the name of a saint or of some other person distinguished for holiness be chosen, for this will be of a spiritual advantage to the child and an edification to others.

—*Codex Iuris Cononici,* Rome, 1917

ITALIAN BATTALION

Traditional Italian-American families adhere to a strict naming procedure brought over from Italy, in which everybody is named after somebody else. Here's how it works:

First son is named after   father's father
First daughter . . . . father's mother
Second son . . . . mother's father
Second daughter . . . . mother's mother
Subsequent sons . . . . father's brothers, in order of age. If you run out, mother's brothers.
Subsequent daughters . . father's sisters, in order of age. When you finish with them, mother's sisters.

This practice radically simplifies the naming decision, especially since, until this generation, most Italian families were so large it was tough to exhaust the entire store of possibilities. It also leads to lots of children with the same names. To prevent too much overlap, variations are permissible and often used, especially for girls' names. Grandma Rosemarie, for instance, may have namesakes called Rose, Maria, Annemarie, Rosanne, and Mary. Grandpa Anthony, whose name cannot be varied as easily, is likely to spawn a veritable legion of Anthonys.

Assimilation, intermarriage, and the trend to smaller families are combining to endanger this sort of name inbreeding. While it's sad to lose such a finely tuned tradition, there is an up side: When you call your child at a family reunion, fifty people don't come running.

ROOTS

Shortly after he took the heavyweight championship from Sonny Liston in 1964, Cassius Clay announced to the world that he had joined the Nation of Islam and was discarding his "slave name" in favor of Cassius X, soon switched to Muhammad Ali. By renaming himself, Ali was in the vanguard of a movement that was to burgeon in the late sixties, when many blacks adopted the Muslim religion and took on—for themselves and for their children—Islamic names. In 1971, basketball star Lew Alcindor—not a Black Muslim but a member of the orthodox Hanafei sect—changed his name to Kareem Abdul-Jabbar. Other black athletes, entertainers, and public figures followed suit.

At the same time, some people were looking back to their African heritage in search of an ethnically valid name, a trend heavily reinforced by the widely seen television miniseries, "Roots," in 1977. Playwright LeRoi Jones became Imamu Amiri Baraka and soon it was not uncommon to hear tribal names like Ashanti and Akuba in the playground. Still other parents chose to honor heroes of black American history. Playwright and actor Douglas Turner Ward, for instance, abandoned his given birth name of Roosevelt in favor of a combination of the names of abolitionist Frederick Douglass and revolutionary slave Nat Turner.

Black parents who wish to pay homage to their past have a vast menu of unusual names from which to choose. Following is a selection of both Arabic and African names.

ARABIC NAMES

Muslim names usually derive from those of the Prophet Muhammad's descendants or immediate family. There are five hundred variations of the name Muhammad itself; taken together they become the most common boy's name in the world. Other popular Arabic names, such as Karim and Kamil, represent the ninety-nine qualities of God listed in the Koran.

G I R L S

AKILAH	KARIDA
AMINA	LEILA
AYASHA	NIMA
BARAKAH	NUMA
FATIMAH	OMA
HABIBAH	RIDA
HATIMA	RIHANA
HINDA	SELIMA
JAMILA	SHAHAR
JINAN	YASMEEN

B O Y S

ABDEL/ABDUL/ ABDULLAH	IBRAHIM
AHMED/AHMAD	JAFAR
ALI	JAMIL
ALLAH	JUMAH
AZIM	KAMALI
DAWUD	KAMIL
FARIO	KARIM
HAKEEM	KASIM
HAMID	MALIK
HANIF	MUHAMMAD and
HASHIM	its variations
HASSAN	OMAR
HUSAIN	RAHMAN

If you have a hundred sons, name them all Muhammad.

—Muslim proverb

AFRICAN NAMES

G I R L S

ABA	ADIA
ABINA/ABENA	AKUBA
ADESINA	AMMA

APRILI
ASIZA/AZIZA
BARIKA
CAMISHA
CHIRIGA
DALILA
FAYOLA
HASINA
IMENA
JANI
JINA
KANIKA
KATURA

KAYA
KIAH
LAYLA
NEEMA
OBA
RASHIDA
SHANI
TABIA
TARANA
TISA
YABA
ZAHARA

B O Y S

ABASI
ADOM
AGU
AJANI
ASHANTI
ASHON
AYANA
AZIZI
BELLO
BEM
KAYIN

KITO
KOSEY/KOSSE
KWAMIN
KWASI
LADO
MASUD
ODION
OKO
RUDO
SUDI
TANO

He walked there now . . . thinking of names. Surely, he thought, he and his sister had some ancestor, some lithe young man with onyx skin and legs as straight as cane stalks, who had a name that was real. A name given to him at birth with love and seriousness. A name that was not a joke, nor a disguise, nor a brand name. But who this lithe young man was . . . could never be known. No. Nor his name.

—Toni Morrison, *Song of Solomon,*
Alfred A. Knopf, 1977

Wednesday Is Full of Woe

The Ashantis in West Africa name their children according to the day of the week on which they are born. Each day is believed to signify a certain temperament—for example, Monday boys are quiet and obedient, Wednesday boys fiery and aggressive. And sure enough, more offenses are committed by Wednesdays than by any others, with very few delinquents born on (and so named) Monday.

FUNNY, YOU DON'T SOUND SCOTTISH

If you want to give your child a name that reflects your ancestral roots, you should be certain whereof you name. Matching up a name with its country of origin is trickier than it might seem: Many assumptions, beliefs, and, yes, even listings in name books, are just plain wrong. Test your own knowledge of the ethnic derivations of names by taking the following quiz. Match up the name on the left with the correct origin from the list at right:

1. CHITA   a. English
2. IRVING   b. Scottish
3. JENNIFER   c. Welsh
4. DUANE   d. Irish
5. LEROY   e. French
6. JOCELYN   f. German
7. SAPPHIRE   g. Hebrew
8. TIFFANY   h. Greek

The correct answers are: 1,a; 2,b; 3,c; 4,d; 5,e; 6,f; 7,g; 8,h. Surprised? Irving doesn't sound Scottish, you say? Sapphire doesn't sound Hebrew, Tiffany doesn't sound Greek?

Well, they're not the only ones. For specifics, consult the following list, with origins in alphabetical order, bearing in mind that tracing derivations is a very complex business, what with much of the population of the British Isles speaking French for hundreds of years during the Middle Ages, German names often being Teutonic versions of Latin ones, and so on. We have tried to offer examples here on which there is a general consensus of authoritative opinion.

ENGLISH NAMES

GIRLS

AUDREY
BEVERLY
CHITA (from the
   Middle English
   chitte, meaning
   kitten)

DARLA
HEATHER
SCARLETT
TYNE
VIOLA
WANDA

BOYS

BRANDON
BURTON
DARRYL
DENVER

IRWIN
MILTON
MORTON
SEYMOUR

SHELDON   TODD
SHERMAN   WAYNE

FRENCH NAMES

G I R L S

AMY   FLANNERY
BONNIE   MALLORY
CHARLOTTE   MARGERY
CHERYL   MARION
CLAIRE   ROSALIE
FAY

B O Y S

CASE   MORTIMER
CHANDLER   OLIVER
CURTIS   ORSON
GARRISON   RUSSELL
LEROY   TYSON
MASON   VERNON

GERMAN NAMES

G I R L S

ADELAIDE	LORELEI
EMMA	RUE
IRMA	SILVER
JOCELYN	

B O Y S

ALBERT	GILBERT
ARNOLD	HENRY
BERN(H)ARD	HERBERT
CONRAD	RICHARD
GEOFFREY	WILLIAM

GREEK NAMES

G I R L S

CATHERINE	ELEANOR
CHLOE	EUNICE
CORA	IRENE
CYNTHIA	IRIS
DORIS	LOIS
DOROTHY	LYDIA

MARGARET	SOPHIA
MELANIE	THERESA
MELISSA	TIFFANY
PHYLLIS	ZOE

B O Y S

ANDREW	JEROME
BASIL	LINUS
CHRISTOPHER	LUKE
DAMIAN	MYRON
EUGENE	PETER
GEORGE	PHILIP
GREGORY	STEPHEN
ISIDORE	THEODORE
JASON	TIMOTHY

HEBREW NAMES

G I R L S

ABIGAIL	KEZIA(H)
BEULAH	MAHALIA
DINAH	RAPHAELA
ELIZABETH	SAPPHIRE
JEMIMA	SHARON
JESSICA	SUSAN

B O Y S

ABNER	JETHRO
AMOS	JOHN (a contraction
ASHER	of the Hebrew name
CALEB	Johanan)
EMMET	JOSEPH
ETHAN	OMAR
GABRIEL	RAPHAEL
JARED	TOBIAS
JESSE	

IRISH NAMES

G I R L S

GRANIA	STACEY
MONA	UNA
MURIEL	

B O Y S

BARRY	DESMOND
DARREN	DUANE
DERMOT	TYRONE

SCOTTISH NAMES

G I R L S

BLAIR	MAISIE
CRYSTAL (first used as a boy's name)	RONA

B O Y S

BOYD	KENNETH
BRUCE	KYLE
IRVIN/IRVING	MAXWELL
JAMIE	MONROE
KEITH	MURRAY

WELSH NAMES

G I R L S

CARON	JENNIFER
ENID	MEREDITH
GLADYS	MORGAN
GLENDA	RHONDA
GWEN/GWENDOLYN	WINIFRED

B O Y S

CONWAY	LLOYD
CRAIG	OWEN
DEWEY (Welsh form	REESE
of Hebrew David)	TREVOR
GLENN	VAUGHAN

When I was a kid, I didn't know anybody named Heather or Joshua. In my neighborhood, boys had solid workmanlike names: Stanley, Chester, Walter, Norbert, Albert, Henry, or Joe. Girls had in-the-kitchen names like Bertha, Dorothy, Helen, Mildred, Eleanor, Mary, Lucille, and Gertrude.

But today, it's not unusual to find people with monikers like Heather Potkowski, Kevin Bongiorino, Danielle Goldberg. No wonder young people grow up confused about who they are.

—Mike Royko, *Chicago Tribune* syndicated column,
June 12, 1987

NAMES THAT NEVER CROSSED THE OCEAN

We all know about Mario and Olga and Otto, the names that have successfully immigrated and integrated into our national stockpot of names. But there are many others that have never really made it across the big pond and you might want to consider these in light of your own ethnic heritage.

ENGLISH NAMES

GIRLS

ALTHEA	KIMBRA
ARAMINTA	LIVIA
BRYONY	OTTILIE
ISMAY	SIDONY(IE)
KARENZA/KERENSA	TAMSIN

B O Y S

ALARIC	INIGO
ARLEY	IVO
BEVIS	OZIAS
CRISPIN	PEREGRINE
DUNSTAN	TORQUIL

FRENCH NAMES

G I R L S

BICHETTE	LUCIENNE
CELINE	NICOLETTE
CHANTAL	ODILE
ELIANE	SOLANGE
FABIENNE	SYLVIE

B O Y S

ALAIN	GIRAUD
BENOIT	LAZARE
DIDIER	LUC
ETIENNE	REMI
FABRICE	THIERRY

GERMAN NAMES

G I R L S

AMALIE	LENI
ANNELISE	MINA
CAROLA	PINA
GISELA	SANNA
JAKOBINE	TRESA

B O Y S

BARTOL	KASPAR
CLAAS	KASS
DIETER	MATHIAS
ESRA	WOLF/ULF
JORN	ZAN

GREEK NAMES

G I R L S

ALLISTO	JOCASTA
CLIO	KALIOPE
EMALIA	KATINA
HALI	LILIKA
IANTHE	NERISSA

B O Y S

ALEXIOS	KOSTAS
COSMOS	KYROS
DARIUS	THANOS
DINOS	YANNIS
ILIAS	ZENO

HEBREW NAMES

G I R L S

ADIRA	LAILI(E)
ARE(L)LA	MORIA(H)
AZIZA	NEORA
DEVORA	NITZANA
KIRYA	RAVIVA

B O Y S

AZRIEL	ORI
BOAZ	SHAUL
DOV	YAAKOV
LAEL	YOEL
LEVI	ZIV

IRISH NAMES

G I R L S

ANNORA	JUNO
BEDELIA	KEELIN
BRENNA	MAEVE
BRETTA	ORLA
FIANNA	SORCHA

B O Y S

CARRICK	EAMON
CURRAN	KERN
DECLAN	KIL(L)IAN
DERMOT	LIAM
DOUGAL	RONAN

ITALIAN NAMES

G I R L S

ANINA	LETIZIA
BENEDETTA	LIA
CHIARA	MARZIA
CLELIA	OTTAVIA
FABIANA	PAOLINA

B O Y S

ADRIANO
ALESSO/ ALESSIO
AMADEO
AURELIO
DAMIANO

ELIO
FABIO
LUCIO
SANDRO
TADDEO

POLISH NAMES

G I R L S

ANIELA
FRANCISCKA
HALINA
JANA
KAMILLA

KASSIA
LUDVICA
STASHA
TESIA
ZOFIA

B O Y S

ANZELM
FLORIAN
GERIK
JANOS
JAREK

LUKASZ
MAREK
MARIUS
MATEUSZ
TANEK

RUSSIAN NAMES

G I R L S

ALINA	LARISA
DARIJA	LIOLYA
EVVA	TATIANA
GALINA	VARINA
KISA	YELENA

B O Y S

AKIM	LAVRENTI
ALEXI	LUKA
DAVEED	PAVEL
FEODOR	SERGEI
KASIMIR	YURI

SCANDINAVIAN NAMES

G I R L S

AASTA/ASTA (Dan)	KAIA (Dan, Nor)
AILA (Fin)	KARI (Nor)
ANNIKA (Dan)	MARET (Dan)/ MARETE (Nor)
ARLA	MARJA (Fin)
DAGNY (Nor)	VIVEKA (Swe)

B O Y S

ARNE	GALT (Nor)
BARDO (Dan)	JENS (Dan, Swed, and
CLEMENS (Dan)	Nor)
CORT (Dan)	JOREN (Dan)
EERO (Fin)	KAARLO (Fin)
FINN (Nor)	

SCOTTISH NAMES

G I R L S

AILIE/AILI	ISHBEL
BETHIA	LILIAS
CATRIONA	ROBENA
DAVINA	ROSSLYN
GINEVRA	SEONAID

B O Y S

ADAIR	MAGNUS
AULAY	MUNGO
BIRK	NINIAN
KEDDY	TAVIS
LACHLAN	WYNDHAM

SLAVIC/HUNGARIAN NAMES

G I R L S

ANICKA	NEZIKA
DANICA	TESIA
FRANJA/FANIA	VALESCA
JERICA	ZANNA
LIDA	ZORA

B O Y S

DORJAN	KARSTEN
ERNO	KITO
JANOS	ODON
JENO	PIOTR
KAROLY	VILMOS

SPANISH NAMES

G I R L S

CLEMENTINA	MELISENDA
EULALIA	NELIA
LEYA	NILDA
MARISOL	SARITA
MELIA	SERAFINA

B O Y S

ALEJO	LEANDRO
AMADO	MATEO
CLAUDIO	ORLANDO
ENZO	SABINO
ESTEBAN	TADEO

WELSH NAMES

G I R L S

CARYS/CERYS	LLINOS
DERYN	MORWENNA
EIRIAN	NERYS
GWYNFOR	RHIAN/RHIANNON
JESTINA	RHONWEN

B O Y S

BRYNMOR	ILAR
EMRYS	IOLO
GARETH	RHODRI
GLYN	RHYS
GWILYM	SAYER

INTO THE POOL

Some foreign-born celebs—most of them in the movies—have added their names to our national reservoir. Several of their names have gained widespread popularity, while others have seen only occasional use. The Names who have inspired these names include:

F E M A L E

ANOUK Aimee
BRIGITTE Bardot
BRITT Ekland
CLAUDETTE Colbert
DANIELLE Darrieux
DENISE Darcel
ELKE Sommer
GINA Lollobrigida
GLYNIS Johns
GREER Garson
GRETA Garbo
HAYLEY Mills
HEDY Lamarr
ILONA Massey
INGER Stevens
INGRID Bergman
LIV Ullmann
MARLENE Dietrich

MARTINA Navratilova
MELINA Mercouri
MICHELE Morgan
MOIRA Shearer
NADIA Comaneci
NASTASSUA Kinski
PALOMA Picasso
PETULA Clark
POLA Negri
SAMANTHA Eggar
SHEENA Easton
SIGNE Hasso
SIMONE Signoret
SIOBHAN McKenna
SONJA Henie
SOPHIA Loren
VIVECA Lindfors

M A L E

ALAIN Delon
ALISTAIR Cooke
BASIL Rathbone
BJÖRN Borg
CLIVE Brook
DIRK Bogarde
DYLAN Thomas
ELIA Kazan
EMLYN Williams
ERROL Flynn
MARCELLO
   Mastroianni

MIKHAIL
   Baryshnikov
NICOL Williamson
NOEL Coward
OMAR Sharif
PABLO Picasso
RAUL Julia
REX Harrison
SEAN Connery
TREVOR Howard
ZUBIN Mehta

FAMILY TIES

YOU SAY MARIA, I SAY MARYA; LET'S CALL THE WHOLE THING OFF

One of the few advantages of single parenthood must surely be that you get to choose your child's name all by yourself. When you become enchanted with Flora, there's no one around who will say, "Sounds like someone who sells violets in an alley." When you decide absolutely on Kevin, nobody pretends to gag, saying, "Forget it. I went to school with a Kevin who had bad breath." You don't have to deal with anyone wanting to name your child Rudolph after his great-grandfather or Sabra after the heroine of her favorite novel.

However, most people go into parenthood in pairs, and most couples choose their baby's name together. While having a child may, more than any other event, make you and your mate feel as one, choosing the child's name can highlight how separate you really are. Each of you brings your own associations, family history, ethnic background, taste, and imagination to the naming of a child. Attempting to merge all those elements and arrive at a name you both love can sometimes seem as futile as trying to predict your child's genetic makeup.

Some couples avoid wrangling over names by agreeing beforehand that one partner—usually the wife—will choose the children's names. Other husbands and wives split the selection process: He chooses the boys' names and she selects the girls', for instance, or she picks a name for the first child and he decides on the second. This sort of division of mental labor is usually found in couples who divide other kinds of decisions: He decides how to spend the money and she decides which laundry detergent to use, for example. In other words, it's old-fashioned.

Modern dads quite rightly expect an equal voice in choosing the name of the baby whose bottom they're going to diaper half the time, as do modern moms, who will be footing half the baby-sitter's salary. In addition, the fact that couples are marrying—and having children—later in life complicates the naming decision: The longer the separate "past" each partner has, the more potential for disagreement about names. In this case, names with happy old associations can be even more of a no-no than those with unpleasant ones. Resist the urge to commemorate that wonderful weekend you had in Capri five years ago with Carlo or Carlotta.

Some couples attempt to get a jump on the naming-decision process by beginning discussions long before they have a nine-month deadline, even before they have cemented their status as a couple. Names for potential children can become a symbolic turning point in a courtship. "My boyfriend says we can't even talk about getting married until I agree to name our first son Bill," one woman told us. To him, Bill is the epitome of a good, solid name, like "My

Boy Bill" in *Carousel*; to her, it's the retarded title character in the Mickey Rooney film. Wedding plans are still on hold.

Another couple, married for three months, takes long drives in the country to discuss names for their hypothetical child. "My husband likes the name Harry," says the woman. "Everybody in my family thinks it sounds really awful, like a janitor or something."

And a couple who argued about their son's name throughout the pregnancy were shocked in the delivery room by the arrival of a daughter. The husband's first words upon her birth: "Well, I guess that settles the Henry question." While it may have rendered moot their months-long argument over whether the name Henry sounded wimpy or strong, it introduced another question: what to name a girl.

Is there a way to sidestep all this angst in your search for a mutually satisfying name? Part of the solution lies in understanding the problem.

First, you should realize that issues such as differing associations to the names of family members, childhood friends and classmates, and past loves can never truly be resolved: If you went to school with a wonderful Tracy and your mate knew a terrible one, neither of you will ever be able to shake the association.

Differences in taste are stickier. You'll find that if you and your spouse tend to agree on style in clothes, furniture, music, and movies, you'll have an easier time agreeing on a name, or at least coming up with a group of names from which to choose. If, on the other hand, you're one of those couples who battle to the death over whether to buy an antique or a high-tech couch, you may be facing the same kind of fashion issue over choosing a name.

It helps to be aware that picking a name can uncover deep-seated issues of masculinity and femininity. A man may push for macho boys' names and ultrafeminine girls' names; a woman may push for ambisexual names for either. Obviously, what's at stake here is more than a name; it encompasses how you envision your son or daughter, and how you view the sexes in general.

How you see yourself vis à vis your own name can also breed disagreement between you and your mate. Growing up as a Ruth, say, may make you want to give your child a bouncy, fashionable name, while your husband, Jody, may wish to counter his own experience by choosing a name that's classic and grown-up.

While understanding all these problems may not make them go away, it can spark more enlightened naming discussions. Here are some concrete things you can do to arrive at a name that's an optimum choice for both of you:

Talk about issues like image and sexuality before you talk about names: What do you each hope for in a child? Is your fantasy child energetic or studious, "all-boy" or gentle, feminine or tomboy? Coming to agreement on these matters, or at least getting them out in the open, can help when you're choosing a name—not to mention raising your child.

Rule out all names of ex-girlfriends and ex-boyfriends: No matter how much you like the name Jill, do not proceed with it if your husband had a long, torrid affair with a Jill way back when. Do not tell yourself you'll forget: You won't, and neither will he.

Make a "no" list as well as a "yes" list: Most couples only make lists of the names they like; it can help to make lists, too, of the names that are absolutely out for each of you. Include those you'd rule out for personal reasons (the name of the guy who dumped you in high school and the roommate who stole all your clothes) as well as names you simply hate. Agree that neither of you will bring up the names on each other's "absolutely out" lists, no matter how much you like them or how neutral they may be for you.

Avoid using the name selection process as an opportunity to criticize each other's loved ones: When he campaigns for naming your son Morton after his father, this is not an excuse to tell him how much you hate his father, no matter how much you hate the name Morton. Surely you can find enough negative things to say about the name itself without widening the battlefield.

Investigate the reasons for each other's choices: Let's say you love a name your spouse hates. Instead of fighting over the name itself, explore what it is about the name that appeals to you. Figuring out whether you like a name because it's classic, or feminine, or stylish, say, can lead you to other names with the same characteristics that you both may like.

Remember that parenthood is a joint venture: Just as your child will be a unique blend of characteristics from both of you, so should you endeavor to arrive at a name that combines each of your sensibilities and tastes. It will take some enlightened thinking, searching, and negotiating, but that's what this book is all about.

PUTTING THE NAME BEFORE THE BABY

In this age of amniocentesis and ultrasound, many parents have the option of knowing their baby's sex—and thus making a firm decision on a name—long before his or her arrival.

While these medical advances have been a boon for mothers and babies alike, and knowing your child's sex can cut the work of choosing a name in half, we nevertheless caution against telling the world your child's gender and name months before his or her actual arrival.

Announcing in mid-pregnancy that a boy named Dawson is waiting to be born can have a dampening effect on his entrance into the world. For one thing, other people tend to draw a more or less complete picture of little Dawson's looks and personality, based on his name and their knowledge of his parents, long before they get a chance to meet him! For another, you may find that other people are actually less eager to meet him. Instead of waiting by the phone for news of your baby's sex and name, they may receive your announcement with a bored, "Oh, Dawson's finally here."

The only real advantage we can cite for sharing your child's name before his birth is not really that much of a plus: People can give you shower gifts of little T-shirts with Dawson spelled out on the back.

MAUDE: No beautiful names, okay? Not Nicholas or Christopher or Adam or Jonathan.

ROB: Or Jennifer or Gwyneth or Cherish or Innocence.

MAUDE: And no politics, right? Not America or . . . Peace and Freedom . . . just short and to the point . . . Joe, Gus, Eddie. Not Edward, Eddie.

ROB: Sue, Pat—American Bandstand names, right? So it's settled. If it's a girl, it's Tallulah No-Nukes Salinger.

MAUDE: And if it's a boy, it's Bartholomew Zachary Save-the-Whales Chastity-Belt Salinger.

—Micki and Maude, 1984

In Search of a Girl's Name

. . . Jane stroked the pale brown down on the baby's head. "What does she look like to you? She looks like a Miranda to me."

"No."

"Samantha? Christiana?"

"No exotic names."

"Those aren't exotic. How about Gwendolyn?"

"How about Mary?"

"Are you serious, Nick? . . . Mary Cobleigh. It sounds like a barmaid. But Maria might not be bad . . ."

"Too Catholic. . . ."

"How about Tuttle? . . ."

"I hate that," Nicholas said. "I keep meeting all these girls named Heywood and Lockhart and they always had dumb-bunny nicknames. Although . . . I sort of like Heissenhuber Cobleigh. It has a distinguished ring to it. A fine old name. A noble—"

"If you don't stop I'll put Tammy on the birth certificate."

"I've got it, Jane!"

"This should be terrific."

"Dorothy."

"Even John would be better than that. . . ."

"Come on, now. We need a nice, plain, pretty name. Caroline."

"It sounds like we're copying the Kennedys."

"All right. Ann."

". . . A little too simple. Even with an e."

"Elizabeth."

"I like that," Jane said. "But . . . she doesn't look like an Elizabeth."

"If you name her Zelda then she'll look like a Zelda."

"No, she won't. . . . Let me think. Olivia and Abigail are out. And Winifred. . . . I know," Jane said. "Victoria."

"Victoria?"

"Victoria Cobleigh. It's a little regal, but that's okay. . . . What do you think?"

"You're not going to call her Tory, are you?"

"No! Maybe Vicky, if she's athletic and energetic like you. But otherwise just beautiful, elegant, gorgeous, adorable, sweet, cuddly—"

"Victoria."

—Susan Isaacs, *Almost Paradise,* Ballantine, 1984

BABY, JR.

The easiest solution to the question of what to name a baby boy is to simply repeat the father's name, appending to it the letters Jr. Although this practice is fading out of fashion, it does have certain advantages: a direct link with a progenitor, the pride that goes with carrying on a family name.

But the disadvantages can outweigh the benefits. The child may well feel he's inheriting an identity along with a name, that he's merely a paler shadow of his father, that he will always be number two.

If a boy is actually addressed by the same name as his father, countless confusions will arise, from the most obvious, such as "Which Donald do you want, Big Donald or Little Donald?" on the phone, and fathers and sons opening (and reading) each other's mail, to more subtle ones, like mother having to call the two most important males in her life, husband and son, by the same name.

On the other hand, if the child is called Junior, he is somewhat dehumanized, almost like being referred to as a number, and a lesser number than his father at that. More common is for the child to be known by a familiar, childish form of the name, a practice that spawns its own perils. Dad is Don and junior is Donny, forever locked by his name into an adolescent (or younger) image of himself that persists long after he leaves home. Or, even worse, he might be known to the world as Bud, Buster, Butch, Sonny, Skip, or Chip.

Giving a boy the same name as his father and grandfather—making him a III—is a somewhat different issue. On the positive side, it could be argued that you're carrying on a family tradition rather than purely indulging in egotism. And honorable WASP nicknames for IIIs—Tripp, Tre, or Trey—are not quite as humiliating as the ones many juniors are saddled with. On the down side, little Frederick or Albert the third has the image of not one but two grown-up men to live up to, with a fairly strong (and potentially overwhelming) mandate to carry on the family tradition.

Only one president in the history of the United States has been a junior—James Earl Carter, Jr., who, as we all know, insisted on being known by his childhood nickname of Jimmy. Gerald Ford was born Leslie Lynch King, Jr., but his name was changed when he was adopted by his stepfather. Relatively few juniors are to be found among high achievers in sports or the fine arts. However, there are lots of military men, junior grade.

How to avoid the pitfalls of juniordom and still name your son after his father? You could go the royal route and name him Donald Dalton Duckworth II. Or the child could be given a different middle name, say Donald Duncan Duckworth, be called Duncan by the family, and later sign his memos D. Duncan Duckworth. But before taking this approach, remember the old saying, "Don't trust anyone who parts his name on the side."

Some juniors who made names for themselves

KAREEM ABDUL-JABBAR (Ferdinand Lewis
Alcindor, Jr.)
MUHAMMAD ALI (Cassius Marcellus Clay, Jr.)
JOSEPH W. ALSOP, Jr.
ARTHUR ASHE, Jr.
HARRY BELAFONTE (Harold George Belafonte, Jr.)
MARLON BRANDO, Jr.
YUL BRYNNER (Taidje Khan, Jr.)
WILLIAM F. BUCKLEY, Jr.
JAMES CAGNEY (James Francis Cagney, Jr.)
JIMMY CARTER (James Earl Carter, Jr.)
LON CHANEY, Jr.
CHARLIE CHAPLIN (Charles Spencer Chaplin, Jr.)
CHUBBY CHECKER (Ernest Evans, Jr.)
VAN CLIBURN (Harvey Lavan Cliburn, Jr.)
JIMMY CONNORS (James Scott Connors, Jr.)
JACKIE COOPER (John Cooper, Jr.)
BILL COSBY (William H. Cosby, Jr.)
HUME CRONYN (Hume Blake, Jr.)
SAMMY DAVIS, Jr.
ROBERT DE NIRO, Jr.
JOHN DENVER (Henry John Deutschendorf, Jr.)
TROY DONAHUE (Merle Johnson, Jr.)
MIKE DOUGLAS (Michael Delaney Dowd, Jr.)
CLINTON EASTWOOD, Jr.
BUDDY EBSEN (Christian Ebsen, Jr.)
DOUGLAS FAIRBANKS, Jr. (Douglas Elton Thomas
Ullman, Jr.)

ALBERT FINNEY, Jr.
LOUIS GOSSETT, Jr.
ALEXANDER M. HAIG, Jr.
WILLIAM RANDOLPH HEARST, Jr.
VAN HEFLIN (Emmett Evan Heflin, Jr.)
HAL HOLBROOK (Harold Rowe Holbrook, Jr.)
WILLIAM HOLDEN (William Franklin Beedle, Jr.)
OLIVER WENDELL HOLMES, Jr.
ROCK HUDSON (Roy Harold Scherer, Jr.)
HENRY JAMES, Jr.
STACY KEACH (Walter Stacy Keach, Jr.)
BUSTER KEATON (Joseph Francis Keaton, Jr.)
MARTIN LUTHER KING, Jr.
ALAN LADD, Jr.
ALFRED LUNT, Jr.
TIP O'NEILL (Thomas P. O'Neill, Jr.)
FESS PARKER, Jr.
TYRONE POWER, Jr.
ROBERT REDFORD (Charles Robert Redford, Jr.)
JASON ROBARDS, Jr.
MICKEY ROONEY (Joe Yule, Jr.)
ARTHUR SCHLESINGER, Jr.
RIP TORN (Elmore Torn, Jr.)
KURT VONNEGUT, Jr.
HANK WILLIAMS, Jr.
WILLIAM WRIGLEY, Jr.
FRANK ZAPPA (Francis Vincent Zappa, Jr.)
EFREM ZIMBALIST, Jr.

OSCAR HAMMERSTEIN II
LEE MAJORS (Harvey Lee Yeary II)
JACK LEMMON (John Uhler Lemmon III)
EDWIN MEESE III
CLIFF ROBERTSON (Clifford Parker Robertson III)
TOM SMOTHERS (Thomas Bolyn Smothers III)
ADLAI STEVENSON III
LOUDON WAINWRIGHT III

Junior spacemen

Although it isn't a written requirement, being a junior certainly seems to help one's chances of getting into the space program. Juniors who have been launched include:

EDWIN E. ALDRIN, Jr.
CHARLES BASSETT II
GUION S. BLUFORD, Jr.
CHARLES F. BOLDEN, Jr.
ROY D. BRIDGES, Jr.
CHARLES CONRAD, Jr.
L. GORDON COOPER, Jr.
CHARLES M. DUKE, Jr.
JOHN H. GLENN, Jr.
RICHARD F. GORDON, Jr.
FRED W. HAISE, Jr.
HENRY W. HARTSFIELD, Jr.
ROBERT H. LAWRENCE, Jr.
JAMES A. LOVELL, Jr.

THOMAS K. MATTINGLY II
ELLIOT SEE, Jr.
WALTER M. SCHIRRA, Jr.
BREWSTER H. SHAW, Jr.
ALAN B. SHEPARD, Jr.
JOHN L. SWIGART, Jr.
EDWARD H. WHITE II

. . . . In the world of juniors, I was one of the lucky ones. I was never called "Junior" as a nickname. I knew one Junior for years without ever knowing his real name. He and other Juniors will tell you that Junior is their real name and sign it that way on a greeting card or a letter. These are the guys people probably have in mind when they ask me if I have a fragile sense of identity because of my juniorhood. . . . I think that when I was named for my father, the intention was that my name not be simply a utile thing, not be just a handy sound to summon a boy when the garbage needs to be taken down. When a child is named, it is an attempt to define the child. And my definition is my father. I thank my parents for their vote of confidence and I hope I live up to my name. . . .

—Rafael A. Suarez, Jr., "Being a Jr.," *The New York Times Magazine,* April 6, 1986

SIBLING NAMES
(FOR FIRST-TIME PARENTS ALSO)

If you're having your second, third, fourth child or beyond, you have probably already experienced the inherent difficulties and dilemmas involving sibling names. Ideally, the names you choose for later children should "go with" the name you picked for your first child: They should be harmonious in rhythm and style. At the same time, names of later children should be different enough from the first child's name to avoid confusion. Yes, there are families with a Jane and a Jean, a Larry and a Harry, an Ellen and an Eleanor, but the resulting mix-ups do not seem worth the cuteness.

The real problem with sibling names arises because most parents don't consider later names when they choose the first. But the first choice sets the pattern, narrowing future options. Here's how it works:

Because we have personal experience with this one, let's say you decided to name your first child, a girl, Rory. Good enough, but now you're about to have your second. Names that rhyme are out: Goodbye Laurie, Corey, Glory, Maury, Tory, et al. So too with similar-sounding names: everything in the Rose family, the Mary family, the Doria group, the Lauras, Coras, Noras, and Floras, not to mention Larry, Gerry, Terry; Rowen, Rourke, Rollo. You get the idea.

Also, because Rory is such a distinctively Celtic name, it would sound odd with a name from a different ethnic background. Rory and Francesca won't do, for example. In terms of image, Rory is clearly a High-Energy name. Would it be fair to pair her name with one from the Intellectual Power group? Would a little sister named Ruth, for example, always feel bookwormish by contrast; would Rory, conversely, feel flighty in comparison? Another consideration is the name's ambisexuality. Choosing a sister's name from the Feminine or Feminissima group—Angelica, for instance, or Melissa—might not only sound discordant but could make the two girls feel differently about their sexuality. And if the sibling is a boy, giving him an ambisexual name could make matters even more confusing. A girl named Rory with a brother named Ashley? It just wouldn't work. Finally, Rory is a somewhat unusual name, and a more classic choice for a brother or sister could also strike the wrong chord. Rory and Jane? Rory and John? Somehow, they just don't belong together.

Further complications set in if you have changed your ideas about names after living with your real live first choice for a few years. You may regret choosing an ambisexual name like Rory because of the confusion over whether the child was a boy or a girl, and may also wish you had chosen a more common name that was easier for the child to pronounce and for others to understand. You may really want to name your second child Jane or John, and yet not feel comfortable with those choices.

The point of all this is to encourage you to consider future possibilities when you're choosing the name of your first child. If your two favorite names are Anna and Hannah, for example, realize that picking one now rules out the other forever. When you're deciding among several names, consider the future implications of each. Imagining which names might follow for other children may help you narrow the field.

What, in particular, works and what doesn't? Without taste or value judgments on the specific names, we can tell you some instances of sibling names we're familiar with that do work. Jane and William, for instance, or Sam and Lily. Both pairings are good because, for one, the girls' names are clearly feminine and the boys' clearly masculine. The style is consistent: fashionable, but not to the point of cliché. And the names sound well together but do not sound confusingly alike. Another good brother-and-sister combo is Elizabeth and Charles, called Libby and Charley. Both are classic names that happen to be in style now, and both nicknames are gently old-fashioned, more compatible than, say, Liza and Chuck would be.

Two brothers whose names catch the right rhythm are Felix and Leo. Both are traditional names—saints' names in fact—that, because they haven't been widely used for some years, have an appealingly offbeat quality. The x and the o endings provide different but equally unusual sounds for the two names, and they are further related by both being feline.

We know a family of three girls named Melissa, Danielle, and Lauren. Their mother wanted to name the third daughter Patricia. But the classic Patricia—or Pat or Patti—simply did not sound like the sister of the trendier Melissa and Danielle, so Lauren she became.

Fictional children, whose writer "parents" choose all the names at once for kids years apart in age, are often models for name groups that catch the appropriate rhythm: Mallory, Alex, and Jennifer Keaton of television's "Family Ties," for instance. All euphonic, trendy names, although the mainstream Jennifer stands out a bit, reflecting her TV parents' move toward comformity. When the fictional Keaton mom was pregnant with a fourth child, Jennifer suggested the names Charo and Shecky, but no one took her ideas seriously. The baby was called, predictably, Andrew.

One of the most discordant fictional sets of sibling names in recent times has been Hannah and her sisters, Holly and Lee, in the Woody Allen film. While the movie was hailed as a triumph for its realism, these three names were anything but believable. The only thing that relates Hannah and Holly is the initial H; beyond that,

Hannah is a Biblical name, old world and serious, while Holly is an invented name not used at all until this century and not widely until the 1960s. Holly and Lee, meanwhile, are more consistent in style and tone, but echo each other in sound. Hannah and Lee sound more like sisters than Hannah and Holly do, but even so, Hannah and Leah would have been closer to the mark. In fact, Hannah, Helen, and Leah sound as if they were born of the same parents, while Hannah, Holly, and Lee sound like three women who just happen to be at the same party, which may have been Woody Allen's intention after all.

When the name of a fictional character breaks rank with those of his or her siblings, there's usually some symbolism involved. The classic case is *Little Women*'s Meg, Jo, Beth, and Amy. Even if you haven't read the book, guess which one was the tomboy with ambitions greater than her sisters'.

So too in real life, where the child with a name that is "different" from those of his brothers and sisters may also feel different in spirit. We know of a family with four children named Mary, Christopher, Nicole, and Alexandra. It's clear here too which one considers herself the odd child out.

If you already have your first child and are choosing a name for a sibling, keep the following guidelines in mind:

Don't be cute: No rhymes, sound plays, precious pairings. Resist the temptation, for example, to name Daisy's sister Maisie, Darcy, or Hyacinth.

Don't fall into the same initial trap: A trend of the fifties and sixties was to choose sibling names all starting with the same letter. Sometimes, parents didn't consider the consequences if they had chosen to start with the letter E and happened to have, say, five boys.

Edward was fine for the first, Eliot okay for the second, but by the birth of their fifth son they were stuck with choices like Earl, Elmer, and Egbert. While few parents have five children today, the same-initial trend should be avoided as dated and overly precious.

Do maintain consistency of style, image, sex, and tradition: This rule is to be interpreted loosely, but, as detailed in the example of Rory, sibling names should ideally stay in the same, well, family.

Be careful about sexual distinctions: If you choose a boyish name for your daughter, and later have a son, go with a boy's name that is clearly masculine. So too if you give your boy an ambisexual name; both he and his little sister will fare better if her name is distinctly feminine. The names of same-sex children should not have widely divergent sexual images: Bruno's brother shouldn't be named Blair, for instance, nor should Belinda's sister.

Avoid using two names with the same nickname: This problem usually crops up when parents, hoping for a junior, despair at the third girl and name her Roberta or Christina or Geraldine. She then becomes Bobbie or Chris or Gerry. When her long-awaited little brother is born five years later, he is named Robert or Christopher or Gerald. Try as the parents might to prevent it, they may end up with a Bobbie and a Bobby, Chris and Chris, or Gerry and Gerry, in addition, of course, to Bobby, Chris, or Gerry Sr. The trend toward smaller families has headed off most occurrences of this problem in recent years, but it still happens. If you're entirely positive that if you ever have a boy you'll name him Christopher, don't name a girl Christina when you give up hope on having a son, or vice versa. Accidents do happen.

Double trouble

Twins offer a rare opportunity for parents to choose two related names at the same time, but also multiply the difficulties inherent in sibling names. With twins, it can be more tempting to use rhyme, sound play, and same-initial names, but in our opinion pairings like Eddie and Teddy, Faith and Charity, or Charles and Charlene should be relegated to a time capsule. While same-initial names that are clearly distinct from one another, such as Ross and Rachel, twin children of Jane Pauley and Garry Trudeau, are okay, different-initial names that are consistent in style and tone are preferable.

Some celebrity examples that work: Cybill Shepherd's Ariel and Zack; Meredith Baxter-Birney and David Birney's Mollie and Peter; Ron Howard's Paige and Jocelyn. In all these cases, the names are distinct from each other yet make a harmonious pair—exactly what most parents would want for the twins themselves.

Two examples of twin names that don't work—Debby Boone's Gabrielle and Dustin, and Mia Farrow and André Previn's Matthew and Sascha—fall short for the same reason: Each set has one sexually distinct name and one ambi name. Based on the names alone, one would surmise that they were both boy-girl pairs. In fact, Gabrielle and Dustin are twin girls, and Matthew and Sascha are both boys.

Whatever the sex of the children, twin names should present a compatible image. As detailed in the discussion on sibling names, pairings like Gigi and Walter or Candida and Jennifer are too discordant. Gigi's twin would better be named, perhaps, Barnaby; Walter's sister might be Margaret; Candida's twin could conceivably be called Isabella; and Jennifer's obvious other half is—who else?—Jason.

Ariel and Zack get their birth certificate first names [Molly and Cyrus] from Cybill's great-great-grandparents. Their middle names come right out of a baby book "from A to Z," says Cybill.

—*People* magazine, December 21, 1987

WHOSE NAME IS IT, ANYWAY?

It is Thanksgiving. You and your sister-in-law, both newly pregnant, are sitting with the rest of the family around the table. Talk turns to names.

"If we have a boy, of course he will be Richard the Third," says your sister-in-law, smiling sweetly at your father. Your brother, Richard Jr., beams.

You, on the other hand, choke on your cranberry sauce. Ever since you were a little girl, you've wanted to name your first son Richard. Besides being your father's name, it's also your husband's father's name, your brother's name, and your favorite boy's name in all the world.

"We were planning on Richard, too," you manage to sputter.

"You can't have it," booms your brother. "Clearly it's our name."

"There's room for two Richards in the family," you reason. "We'll just use different nicknames."

"That's stupid," your brother says. "Ricky and Richie?"

"Now, now," soothes your mother. "What if you have girls?"

"Amanda," you and your brother say in unison.

If you and your spouse have proliferating siblings, the issue of who gets to use which names is one you may have to face. And a difficult issue it is. Does a son have absolute dibs on the father's name? Is there room in a family for two cousins with the same name? Is there a pecking order for who gets traditional family names? Is getting there first a good enough reason to usurp somebody else's name? Can you set claims on a name to begin with?

How you answer these questions depends a lot on your individual family. In some families, the oldest son has eternal right to his father's name, even if he never has a son of his own. In others, it's first come, first served, with the understanding that there will be no later duplications. And some families just play catch-as-catch-can, and worry later about how they'll deal with three cousins named, say, Eric.

If you anticipate some name-wrestling within your own family, keep the following tips in mind:

Announce your choices early on: If you have an absolute favorite name you're sure you will use, don't make a secret of it. Planting it in everyone's mind as "your" name can help avoid problems later.

Don't steal someone else's name: We're not talking about naming your baby Letitia, unaware that, on the same day in a different state, your sister is naming her baby Letitia. We're talking about naming your baby Letitia when your sister has been saying since she was fifteen that her fondest wish in life was to have a little girl named Letitia. And your sister is eight months pregnant. And knows she's having a girl.

Avoid carbon copies: Two little Caroline Townsend Smiths in a close-knit family is one too many. If you want to use the same first and middle names that a sibling uses, can you live with a different nickname—Carrie, for instance? Or can you vary the middle name, so that, at least within the family, one cousin is called Caroline Townsend and the other, say, Caroline Louise? The only case in which two cousins named Caroline Townsend and called Caroline can work is if they have different last names.

Honor family traditions: If the oldest child of the oldest child in your family is always named Taylor, don't break rank, unless your oldest sibling is a nun, priest, or Gay Rights organizer and formally renounces rights to the name.

Take unintentional, unimportant duplications in stride: We know two sisters-in-law, living across the country from each other, who were pregnant at the same time: Jane due in January and Anne in April. During their annual Christmas Eve phone conversation, Jane said she was sure she'd have a boy, and that they were planning to name him Edward. "That's our name," gasped Anne. "Too bad," Jane said blithely. After a few minutes of intense anxiety, Anne decided Jane was right. Neither had officially "claimed" Edward, nor was it a name with any family significance. It would be as ridiculous to insist that Jane change her choice at the eleventh hour as it would be to deny her own son the name just so it wouldn't duplicate that of a cousin he'd see, at best, once a year. Besides, Jane favored the nickname Eddie, while Anne preferred Ted. P.S.: Due to mitigating circumstances, neither baby was named Edward. They ended up Juliet and Josephine.

NAME IN THE MIDDLE

What of your child's middle name?

The strongest trend today is to give your baby a middle name that has meaning. It might be your maiden name, another family surname, the name of someone close to you, or a name with more personal symbolic meaning. Many firstborn sons who are not juniors are still given their fathers' names as middle names; increasingly, daughters are getting their mothers' first names as middle names.

Another trend, sparked by the new generation of royal babies, is to give your child more than one middle name, à la little Prince William Arthur Philip Louis, to honor all the relatives in one fell swoop.

You may want to balance an unusual first name with a more solid middle name, or vice versa, if you're unsure of your choice and want to give your child an option later. Or perhaps you feel obligated by tradition or family pressure to give your child a name you absolutely hate: Its place is tucked discreetly in the middle.

Still another increasingly popular option is to give your child no middle name at all. A growing number of parents feel that unless a middle name has some personal meaning, it serves no purpose and may border on the pretentious; others feel that a middle name is "wasted" on a girl, who may drop it when she marries, slotting her maiden name in the middle. (With more and more women keeping their original last names after marriage, this argument no longer stands up.)

What is decidedly out of fashion is giving your child a "throwaway" middle name—a euphonic if insignificant bridge between the first and last name. These are the Anns, Sues, and Lees of our childhoods, names that no one particularly liked or cared about, but that sounded right to the fifties ear following Lisa or Barbara or Karen.

Even more passé (except in the South, where the practice has always been beyond fashion) is giving your child a throwaway middle name you don't throw away—naming her Lisa Ann, for instance, and calling her Lisa Ann.

THE NAME BECOMES THE CHILD

Finally comes the day when you hold your real live child in your arms and make a final decision on a real live name. At that point, all the lists you've made, the considerations you've weighed, and the options you've juggled fall by the wayside and you and your child are left with your ultimate choice.

What happens then?

Well, on one hand, the struggle over Miranda vs. Molly seems less crucial in the face of three A.M. feedings, colic, and the high cost of diapers. And it doesn't take very long for your baby's persona to dominate the name, for your baby to become his or her name. For the first two weeks, you may find yourself still calling little Miranda "It"; for the next few, you may feel self-conscious each time you pronounce the name; but a month later you'll find that when you say "Miranda" you don't hear the sound of the name but see instead your child's curved lips and dark curls.

On the other hand, once you've settled on a name, you deal with its myriad implications, often for the first time. You may discover, for instance, that your Aunt Elizabeth is not satisfied to be honored by a mere middle name, that people on the street do not necessarily assume Jordan is a girl, and that friends have to suppress a snicker when you tell them you've named your son Henry.

This may not be fun. This may cause you to retrieve your original lists of possibilities and say to your spouse in the middle of the night, "Maybe we should have named him Michael." And of course, it is possible to change a child's name two days or two months or even two years after you've given it, but it's not easy for many reasons and it's not what we're considering here.

Better than contemplating a name change would be to mull over the fact that choosing one option—in names as in everything else—always means forgoing all others. That the name you've selected inevitably becomes influenced by reality, while the ones you've rejected remain fantasies, entirely pleasant because you alone control them. That in fact if you had chosen Michael, say, you might then be worrying about its ordinariness, might be wishing in the middle of the night that you had gone with something more distinctive like . . . Henry.

Obviously, much of the value of this book is that it helps you anticipate the real world repercussions of a name. And much of the impetus for writing it came from our own experiences and those of our friends in choosing names for children and living with the choices.

One of our friends, for instance, has two children: Emily and Jeremy. "When Emily was born we were living in the country and it seemed like a really special, unusual name," she says. "Then when she was a few months old we moved to the city and I discovered that there were little Emilys everywhere. I felt terrible. I would listen in the playground for other kids named Emily, I would pore over nursery school class lists for other Emilys, and if she was the only Emily I'd feel so relieved. On one hand I feel badly because it seems as if the name is a cliché, but there also aren't as many Emilys as I'd originally feared."

Our friend pinpoints another reason why she was unaware of how widely used the name Emily was (and another reason we wrote this book): "Having a first child I didn't really know any other young parents. I had no idea what people were talking about when they named their kids or what the new style was. My idea of a trendy name was still Barbara or Sue."

What then of Jeremy's name? "That one I haven't had so many problems with," she says, "except that some people keep trying to call him Jerry."

Parents who've chosen less usual names talk of unanticipated problems with pronunciation and comprehension. A little girl named Leigh is sometimes called "Lay"; a child named Hannah is called Anna by some people. One of us has some regrets about calling her daughter Rory because the name is more often understood as Laurie, Corey, Tory, Dory, or even Gloria or Marie than as its rightful self.

Then there's the issue of the child's name vis à vis his or her looks and personality. Many parents wait to make a name choice until they see which of their finalists best fits the child. This makes some sense, but you should be aware that a newborn is not necessarily representative of the five- or twelve-year-old he or she will become. The chubby, noisy infant daughter you name Casey may grow into a dainty, ultrafeminine ballet dancer, while the delicate baby who seems to be the quintessential Arabella may become, ten years later, goalie on the neighborhood boys' hockey team.

This brings us to the flip side of this issue: Children can irrevocably color our perceptions of their names. You undoubtedly have unique feelings about certain names based on the children you know who bear them, and so do we. When we disagreed about whether to include a particular name on a list here, it was usually because we each knew people who brought different things to it: a handsome and irreverent Ralph, for example, vs. a boorish one; an adorable kid named Kermit vs. the frog on TV.

Reading this book can help prepare you for some of a name's eventualities, then, but not for others. You wouldn't be surprised, as our friend was, that Emily is a fashionable name or that some people are bent on using undesirable nicknames. Neither will you be unaware of both the advantages and the complications of giving your child a popular or an unusual name, or that Cameron can also be a girl's name, or that Henry has an intellectual image and so can be perceived by some people as a bit nerdy.

But no one, including you, has ultimate control over the person your child turns out to be. A name can remind you of your hopes and fears way back when childbirth was a point on the horizon, but your child—the one who's laughing or crawling or walking across the room in his own special way—can remind you that Henry by any other name, be it Michael or Melchizedek, would still be your own sweet boy.

INDEX

GIRLS' NAMES

Yaba, 224
Yael, 179, 212
Yaf(f)a, 212
Yasmeen, 222
Yasmine, 148
Yelena, 241
Yolanda, 36, 148
Yona(h), 212
Yvette, 143
Yvonne, 148

Zahara, 224
Zandra, 92, 148
Zane, 92, 179

Zanna, 243
Zara, 64, 92, 113, 148
Zelda, 36, 89, 152
Zelia, 92, 148
Zena, 148
Zenobia, 217
Zia, 148
Zinnia, 28
Zita, 217
Zoe, 60, 62, 78, 92, 113, 148, 231
Zofia, 240
Zora, 243
Zorah, 148

BOYS' NAMES

Aaron, 15, 19, 165, 195, 197, 217
Abasi, 224
Abbott, 11
Abdel, 223
Abdul, 223
Abdullah, 223
Abe, 10, 20, 210
Abel, 33, 165, 217
Abner, 19, 33, 72, 165, 232
Abraham, 210, 217
Achilles, 125
Adair, 242
Adam, 15, 19, 21, 42, 74, 75, 107, 165,
    195, 197, 210, 217, 252
Addison, 11, 75, 108, 179
Adin, 213
Adlai, 70, 88
Adolf, 217
Adolph, 36, 70
Adom, 224
Adrian, 23, 92, 107, 217
Adriano, 240
Agu, 224
Ahmad, 223
Ahmet, 61
Aidan, 19, 67, 165, 179, 217
Ainsley, 170
Ajani, 224
Ajax, 125
Akim, 241
Akuba, 221
Al, 131
Alain, 236, 246
Alan, 130, 162, 179, 190, 210
Alaric, 66, 236
Albert, 88, 162, 217, 230, 234, 255
Aldo, 22
Alec, 19, 112, 113, 165

Alejo, 244
Alessio, 240
Alesso, 240
Alex, 15, 19, 45, 75, 107, 112, 165,
    175, 178, 262
Alexander, 15, 45, 63, 64, 65, 165, 176,
    196, 217
Alexi, 241
Alexios, 238
Alexis, 176, 177, 217
Alfred, 137, 162
Algernon, 170
Ali, 178, 223
Alistair, 23, 92, 246
Allah, 223
Allan, 162, 179, 190
Allen, 162, 179, 190
Allie, 176
Ally, 176
Allyn, 179
Alonzo, 22
Aloysisus, 170
Alvin, 36, 72, 170
Amadeo, 240, 244
Amadeus, 125
Ambert, 170
Ambrose, 31, 217
America, 192, 252
Amias, 217
Amiracle, 42
Amnon, 213
Amon, 213
Amory, 11, 31
Amos, 29, 122, 124, 165, 232
Amyas, 92
Anatol, 92
André, 92
Andrea, 66, 176

ABOUT THE AUTHORS

LINDA ROSENKRANTZ is the author of the novel *Talk* and co-author of *Gone Hollywood* and *SoHo*. The former editor of *Auction* magazine, she now writes a nationally syndicated column on collectibles.

PAMELA REDMOND SATRAN, former fashion features editor of *Glamour*, writes a syndicated column aimed at working parents. Her freelance articles have appeared in numerous publications, including *Self, Elle, Working Mother*, and *The Washington Post*.